Library
Oakland S.U.M.

"Is God a green snake two miles long
(as believed by some aborigines)?"
"Is God no more than the sum total
of the universe?" "Does God really exist?"
These and ninety-seven other
questions confron̳ ̳
chaplain as he ̳
about God in a
students of vari
graduates and ̳
agnostics and a̳
non-Christians.

The chaplain's question: How can he
make God real to these young people?

100 QUESTIONS ABOUT

100 QUESTIONS ABOUT GOD

BY J. EDWIN ORR

A DIVISION OF G/L PUBLICATIONS
GLENDALE, CALIFORNIA, U.S.A.

Second Printing, 1968
Third Printing, 1970
Fourth Printing, 1971

© Copyright 1966 G/L Publications
Printed in U.S.A.

Published by
Regal Books Division, G/L Publications
Glendale, California 91209 U.S.A.

ISBN 0-8307-0014-5

CONTENTS

Chapter 1

IS THERE A GOD?

"The Founding Fathers of the United States of America stated plainly," began the Chaplain, "'We hold these truths to be self-evident, that all men are created equal, that they are endowed by their Creator with certain unalienable rights; that among these are life, liberty and the pursuit of happiness.' Notice that the Founding Fathers attributed our basic human rights to the Creator. God was the starting point of their declaration . . ."

"Excuse me, sir!" interrupted a student. "Is it not fair to say that there are many Americans who would fight for life, liberty and the pursuit of happiness without a thought of God?"

"Undoubtedly," said the Chaplain.

"Would they not say," went on the student, "that their ancestors fought for these rights?"

"Certainly," said the Chaplain. "There was once an Irishman taking a stroll upon a Sunday morning when he encountered an English duke also taking a stroll. Said the duke, 'You're trespassing, my man. This is my property!'

" 'Where did you get it?' asked the Irishman.

" 'From my father!' said the duke.

" 'Where did he get it?' asked the Irishman.

" 'From my grandfather!' said the duke.

" 'Where did he get it?' asked the Irishman.

" 'From my ancestors!' said the duke.

" 'And where did they get it?' asked the Irishman, defiantly.

" 'They fought for it,' said the duke. Said the Irishman, 'I'll fight you for it!' "

The whole group laughed heartily. When the laughter subsided, the Chaplain continued: "We may say that we possess a right to life, liberty, and the pursuit of happiness because we fought for it, but what's to prevent someone else fighting us for it to take our right away? Do we have a title, a clear title, to our rights?"

A hand was raised. "You mean, sir," ventured a young lady, "that we owe our rights to the God who gives the same rights to all men everywhere?"

"Exactly," said the Chaplain. "The right to life, liberty and the pursuit of happiness belonged to the Founding Fathers. But it also belonged to the American Indians, the aboriginal inhabitants of the continent, and to the Negro slaves brought in unwillingly, as well as to the immigrants coming willingly."

There was a reflective pause before a Chinese graduate raised his hand. "You say that these rights were given us by God," he said. "What is your definition of God in this case? Or how can anyone know anything about God? That is my question."

Another hand was raised. "Yes! Look how many ideas of God there are—thousands of them!"

Said the Chaplain, with a smile, "I once met Australian aborigines in Arnhem Land who believed that God was a long, green snake, two miles long. On the other hand, I have met cultured Australians who thought that God was no more than the sum total of the universe. It is a valid question."

He turned to the Chinese from Hong Kong. "Suppose we begin by deciding what God is not. Would you agree that God is not a green snake two miles long?"

"I don't know," said Mr. Liu.

"What would you say he was not?"

"I don't know," persisted the other.

"Would you agree that you are not God?"

"I don't know! I don't think so!"

"Like Euclid," said the Chaplain, "we shall begin with a proposition, then prove or disprove its validity. Listen carefully. God is the only infinite, eternal and unchangeable spirit, the being in whom all things begin, continue and end."

"Where did you get that definition?"

"More or less," explained the Chaplain, "it is condensed from the teaching of Scripture. I suggest that we begin with this definition common to people all over the world belonging to the most widespread faith, which is Christianity."

"Sir," said a student, "my name is Adams, and I am a philosophy student in the university. How do we know that God really exists?"

"An excellent question," said the Chaplain. "Every human being knows by intuition that God exists. This is an insight inherent in man, surely. I think we can say further that it is agreeable to

3

reason, for there are many rational arguments for the existence of God and no one has disproved it by reason. Christians would add that it is an insight verified by revelation and they can testify that it may be confirmed through experience."

"Just one moment, Chaplain," interrupted a young lady. "I have not studied philosophy, so I am asking: What is 'an insight inherent in man'?"

"Thank you, Miss Moore. An insight inherent in man is how we describe a basic truth that is recognized by mankind generally. For example, though difficult to demonstrate, each man knows that he himself exists, and . . ."

"Excuse me," interrupted Mr. Liu, "I have met people who claimed that life is nothing more than an illusion of the five senses. There was a Chinese philosopher who dreamed that he was a butterfly and, in the morning when he wakened up, the dream was so vivid that he did not know whether he was a man dreaming he was a butterfly or a butterfly dreaming that he was a man."

There was a roar of laughter, so much so that the Chaplain intervened.

"I know exactly what Mr. Liu is saying. On the island of Morotai in Indonesia, during the war, one of our planes crashed and several of the crew were badly burned. It was my sad task to bury the dead and comfort the dying. A dying man was wrapped in bandages to the tip of his nose. Not knowing whether he was Protestant, Roman Catholic or Jewish, I began to read the Twenty-third Psalm to him. In the middle of it, he called out loudly, 'Open the window, Doc. It's awful stuffy here.'

"The poor fellow was out in the open air in a temporary casualty ward of the hospital. He had lost his sense of sight, so he had not seen me. He had lost his sense of hearing, so he had not heard me. Presumably, he had lost his sense of taste and smell. He still possessed a little of the sense of touch, for he was in great pain and was under heavy sedation. He lapsed into a coma from which he never recovered.

"While in the coma, without his five senses, what did life mean to him? Nothing! And so, there are people who claim that life is an illusion, a kind of dream."

"Are there educated people in the Western world who claim that life is a dream?"

"Oh, yes!" replied the Chaplain. "Recently, in the University of Oregon, a young lady told me that she did not accept the axiom of existence."

"How did you answer her?"

"I wanted to be careful," said the Chaplain, "not to hurt her feelings or make her the butt of ridicule. I asked: 'What is this at my hand?' She replied: 'A lamp shade.' 'What color?' She replied: 'Pink.' 'What have I just done?' I asked. 'You switched off the light.' 'What have I done now?' 'You switched the light on again.' And so I suggested to her that if we were all dreaming a dream, we were dreaming the same dream, so we assumed that it was true and not an illusion.

"It seems obvious that even the odd objector to the axiom of existence acts as if he believes it to be true. Life may be a dream, but he does not allow that to stop him from ordering lunch."

There was a round of laughter. Then all the thinking students began to phrase other queries in their minds. One identified himself. "My name is Bonelli. I am a student in the field of philosophy.

5

This is my question. If some people claim to be atheists and others agnostics, is it possible to insist as you do that faith in God is an insight common to humanity?"

"Faith in God," said the Chaplain, "is a common human insight, for a great majority of men have recognized a Being or beings on whom they felt themselves dependent. By that I mean that men in every type of culture and every degree of civilization worship some kind of God or gods."

"Just a minute, Chaplain," protested Adams. "What about atheists? What about the atheist?"

"When Chairman Khrushchev was touring the United States, a Russian-American friend of mine watched him carefully on television and in person, trying to lip-read off-the-record conversation. He told me that he was amazed how often the Soviet leader used the name of God in a natural way, such as 'I'm keeping well, thank God!' He quoted an old Russian proverb: 'Whatsoever a man soweth, that shall he also reap.' Of course, though he talks about God like a pious Irishman, he denies believing in God. He says: 'I talk about God, but I am really an atheist. Oh, yes. I am a real atheist. God knows I'm an atheist!'"

There was prolonged laughter.

"But," said an objector, "the atheist does not really believe in God."

"He says so," said the Chaplain. "I knew men who argued in a card-game that they did not believe in God. But when bailing out of a burning airplane, they prayed most fervently. Even the avowed atheist, unable to claim that the idea of God is foreign to the human mind, puts some kind of a substitute in its place. He worships the State, or talks about Life Force or he says that History favors their cause in exactly the same way that the Founding Fathers talked about God."

A quiet young lady suddenly spoke up. "I think that there is plenty of evidence for the idea that everybody knows God intuitively. It's amazing how much time and energy a professing atheist will put into arguing against God. God really bothers him."

"I agree with you, Miss Johnson," said the Chaplain. "But all sorts of people have all kinds of explanations for the universality of belief in a Supreme Being."

"Could it not be said," replied Adams, "that faith in God began through some old philosopher sitting in a cave, through someone's fancied philosophy?"

"Let me answer that," said Helen Johnson. "I did not really and truly believe in God until one night after a storm in the mountains. It was always a hypothetical case with me, until then. I was standing watching the play of lightning in the distance, when all of a sudden the fact of God struck me in a way I have never forgotten. No! No! Faith in God could not have begun through a fancied philosophy, because more often than not it flashes upon the mind as a direct insight and not as a process of reason."

"That's right," said the Chaplain. "One does not need to be a genius to use this insight, for even little children display it; and the range of the insight (if I may describe it that way) far exceeds what anyone by himself could reason out."

"Hold on, Chaplain," said Jack Petersen, an air force lieutenant. "Doesn't every religion just teach its adherents its idea of God? Isn't it a kind of tradition? Could it not be said that faith in God began through someone's traditional teaching?"

"Do you think so, Lieutenant? Just suppose no one had ever mentioned God until this week. Don't you think that people hearing about some mysterious entity called God would be baffled? No! Faith in God could not have begun through a traditional teaching, for unless mankind had first been enlightened by the common insight of God, the doctrine would have been rejected as foreign. In fact, utterly alien. But awareness of God is not foreign. It seems to be common to man."

"Well," objected Bonelli, "it is possible that somebody a long time ago had some kind of what you call a religious experience and that's how it started —you know, like a trance or something. Or maybe a group of cavemen decided to hold a meeting and worship the Great White Spirit or something. Or maybe the idea of God in everybody's mind is a kind of memory worship."

"Excuse me, Pat," said Helen Johnson. "If that were the case, how would a primitive savage having a trance know what he was visualizing? Or what would a group of cavemen think if old Flintstone said: 'Let's all worship God'? Or how would anyone recognize the memory of something happening to others if he could not understand what it was all about? You understand me?"

"What were you trying to say, Pat?" asked the Chaplain. "Maybe faith in God began through someone's learned experience? Miss Johnson is saying—if I may summarize—faith in God could not have begun through learned experience, whether individual encounter or corporate worship or tribal memory. Why? Experience is a result of faith in God, not a cause of such faith."

Another young man identified himself.

"I'm Harry McClelland, and I'm studying at a Bible college. All this talk about God and philosophy leaves me cold. I mean, after all, the Bible just teaches that there is a God and that's that! So why argue about this insight business."

"Harry," said the Chaplain. "Does Scripture itself not teach that faith in God is an insight? Scripture does not argue but instead declares that all men know that God exists . . . 'for all that may be known of God by men lies plain before their eyes . . . his everlasting power and deity have been visible ever since the world began, to the eye of reason, in the things that he has made.' That's Romans, chapter one, verses nineteen and twenty, that I'm reading."

"What version?"

"The New English Bible."

Harry McClelland looked up the verse in the King James translation.

"Okay, okay," he conceded. "I never knew that there was such a verse in the Bible."

The Chinese engineering student raised his hand and added his opinion. "I'm not a Christian. In fact, I thought that Christianity was just another religious superstition, though better than most. But this is what is troubling me. Granted there is a common insight of a Supreme Being. How can what you call Christian experience be said to confirm the common insight of faith in God when in fact many people in the world lack this experience?"

"That troubles me too," said Cynthia Moore.

"Mr. Liu," replied Philip Weber, "I make a hobby of astronomy. I've got my own telescope. Have you ever seen the rings of Saturn? No? Should we deny the existence of Saturn's rings because we have never seen them, yet steadily refuse to use the astronomer's telescope? I don't mean you personally!"

"But why can't an atheist find God?" asked David Adams, impatiently.

Harry McClelland grinned at his big opportunity.

"Many an atheist cannot find God for the same reason that a burglar cannot locate a policeman."

His humor provoked laughter.

"I discover," said the Chaplain quietly, "that intellectual pride and moral disobedience quench the common insight of faith and the Spirit of God by Scripture or godly witnesses rekindles it. Real Christian experience may be found by any who honestly seek. That clinches the argument."

Chapter 2

IF NOT GOD, WHAT?

"Is it possible to prove the existence of God by scientific reasoning?" asked David Adams.

There was a chorus of comment, some saying one thing and some saying the other.

"Order, order," said the Chaplain. "Let's begin somewhere. What would you say, Mr. Liu?"

"If scientific proof is meant," said Mr. Liu, "I contend that the answer is no."

"Are you trying to tell us," asked Cynthia Moore, "that faith in God is unscientific?"

Mr. Liu shot the Chaplain a glance and got an encouraging nod in return.

"Not exactly," said the Chinese, guardedly. "It's like this. If someone said that God was in the next room, what scientific test could we apply to verify the claim? How would you begin—with litmus paper or geiger counter or microscope? Or with something more sophisticated?"

Some nodded with a smile while others thought it through with knitted brows. P. T. Liu glanced at the Chaplain again and continued: "Science cannot measure the specific gravity, or atomic weight or dynamic energy of a spiritual being. Therefore science cannot find God."

"It may also be said," added the Chaplain, "that no branch of science, from astronomy to zoology, contradicts the idea of God. There is no established fact of science or generally accepted theory of science that contradicts the idea of God, as defined."

"What do you mean by that, Chaplain," said Bonelli bluntly.

"Well," said the Chaplain, "I once asked my professor of geology a simple question: 'Is there anything in geology to prevent your believing in God?' He replied equally simply: 'Geology is a study of the crust of the earth. One would not expect to find God among sedimentary rocks!'"

He looked around the group. "Does anyone here take chemistry?"

"I do," said Philip Weber, "and I think that you could say the same thing about chemistry. In fact, I think you'd have to say the same thing about every other science, from astronomy to zoology, as the Chaplain says."

"How about engineering, Peetee?" asked Dave Adams of Mr. Liu.

"There's nothing in engineering against the idea," said he. "Nothing for it, either."

"Nothing for it," corrected the Chaplain, "but a great unanswered question asked by scientists—the question 'Why?'"

"What about the alternatives?" asked Adams. "I

mean, aren't there any alternatives that are likewise not contradicted by science?"

"Like what, Dave?" asked Jack Petersen.

"Well, like chance!" Adams replied.

"Reminds me," began the Chaplain, "of when I was out in the Pacific war. A pilot came to me at Noemfoor and said, 'Chaplain, couldn't things all have happened by chance?' I asked him what he knew about chance and he told me with a grin that he was the squadron expert in shooting craps. So I took out a coin and tossed it and asked him if it were heads or tails.

" 'Now tell me,' I asked, 'what is the chance of getting heads when you toss a coin?'

" 'One out of two,' he replied. I asked him the chance of getting two heads in succession and he replied that it was one out of four. So I asked him . . ."

Helen Johnson interrupted. "Excuse me for appearing dumb," she said, "but how do they work out these fractions? I have never understood how they do it, when they work out the chances of winning a sweepstake. Or," she added embarrassedly, "even why they say 'one out of two' for tossing coins."

The Chaplain left the answer to Petersen who moved quickly to enlighten the helpless sister.

"Well, look, honey," he explained in a big-brotherly manner, "if the Chaplain here arranged a raffle, each one put in a dollar and winner take all, your chance . . ."

There was a burst of laughter at the thought of the Chaplain organizing gambling.

"Your chance," he repeated, "of winning the hundred dollars would be one in a hundred. But your chance of winning twice in succession would be one in a hundred times a hundred or one in ten thousand. See? And the reason your chance of getting heads when you toss a coin is one out of two is because there are only two sides to a coin, heads or tails."

The Chaplain waited for silence to return by conversation to New Guinea. "Then I asked my pilot friend what he knew about dice. He said 'Plenty!' so I asked him the chance of getting six when you roll dice.

"'One out of six,' he replied. For two sixes in succession, he replied that it was 'one out of thirty-six,' and for three sixes in succession, he told me that it was 'one out of two-hundred-and-sixteen,' and for four sixes in succession, he suggested 'One out of one thousand two-hundred and ninety-six.'"

The Chaplain glanced at the girls to see if they were following the calculations.

"And then," he went on, "when I asked him the chance of getting twelve sixes in succession he allowed me to supply the answer:

"'One out of two-billion one-hundred-seventy-six million seven-hundred-eighty-two thousand three-hundred-thirty-six.'"

"How did you get that figure?" asked Cynthia.

"Just multiply," answered Petersen, "six by itself twelve times. That's all."

"Now," concluded the Chaplain, "I asked the pilot what the chance was of getting dice to roll the same way all the time, and he told me simply that it was fantastic. "'Exactly,'" I told him. 'Yet you talk about chance to explain the origins of our universe.'"

The argument was received in silence.

"Let's take something a bit more complicated—take the human body. When your life began, it began as a single cell, which doubled after its fertilization, then became four, eight, sixteen, thirty-two—until it became thousands of cells, millions of cells, billions of cells. But from the beginning these cells seemed to follow some kind of plan, each taking its proper place, each following much the same pattern of organization—until finally you were born. They continue to operate in a complex organization.

"To send a telegram home, I go to a telegraph office, take a telegraph form, write a message, take it to the clerk in attendance, pay a certain amount, and leave the telegram for dispatching. The message is typed, given to a telegrapher to dispatch, sent by cable or radio, and then it is retyped and delivered. Can you imagine all this happening by chance? No, someone had to print those forms, someone had to hire those clerks, someone had to train those telegraphers.

"Compare the human nervous system. If I take a pin and stick it into your leg, a nerve in your leg sends a telegram up to your brain, saying: 'Murphy, you have been stabbed!'" That provoked a roar of laughter. "Then your brain sends a message to your vocal chords urging them to declare something appropriate. Does that happen by chance?"

The Chaplain told the class of an incident on campus at the University of Washington. After his lecture an atomic scientist said to him, "Chaplain, your illustration about the coin and the dice is very interesting, but quite superfluous. In physics, statistically speaking there is no such thing as chance. When one burns hydrogen in oxygen, the result is pure water. When one burns hydrogen in oxygen a hundred times, one gets water a hundred times. When one burns hydrogen in oxygen a thousand times, one gets water a thousand times. And when hydrogen is burned in oxygen a million times, the combustion will form pure water one million times."

"Excuse me," said P. T. Liu. "Is it not true that Professor Miller passed a bolt of electricity through a primeval atmosphere and so obtained amino acids as a result?"

"Yes," said the Chaplain.

"And are not amino acids the building blocks of proteins? Are not proteins the building blocks of life?"

"Yes," said the Chaplain.

"Then could we not say that it was by chance that amino acids were formed and proteins and life? Is not that an argument for chance?"

Before the Chaplain could reply, Philip Weber cut into the dialogue. "Hold on, hold on," he exclaimed. "You've lost me in the shuffle. What was the significance of passing a bolt of electricity through primeval gases? What do you mean?"

"Oh, I can tell you that," replied another science student, Dennison by name. "Miller took some ammonia and methane and other gases like what the earth's atmosphere was supposed to be before the great volcanoes began pouring out their oxygen, and the bolt of electricity was supposed to duplicate the effect of bolts of lightning. The hypothesis was that lightning could account for the production of amino acids."

"True, very true," said the Chaplain, evenly. "Miller deserved a Nobel Prize for his discovery. Scientists are working night and day to try and duplicate life's processes in the laboratory. Each one that makes a breakthrough will deserve a Nobel Prize. What sort of a prize shall we give the original Intelligence that brought about this and a billion other phenomena in the first place?"

"But, Chaplain," protested Adams. "A bolt of electricity! That suggests chance, not plan!"

"My dear Adams," said the Chaplain, tartly, "if you were God and you wanted to create amino acids, would you build a super-cyclotron? Why not use the processes of nature to achieve the immediate and ultimate results? Today, when lightning flashes through our atmosphere of nitrogen, oxygen and other gases, it creates nitrogen compounds which fall in the fields as fertilizers. Is that an argument for blind chance? Is it not an argument for divine purpose? To me, it is all the more marvelous to think God's thoughts after him in the processes of nature. Duplicating steps and studying the design make us realize that the First Great Cause was a clever inventor and mathematician. We would not expect a silly sheep to duplicate the making of amino acids.

"I was once walking along a tropical beach in Australia. I noticed numerous circular tracks in the sand, but decided to attribute them to the action of some lowly sand-worm. Then I noticed a map of Australia outlined in the sand and filled with water. I could have said that this was an accidental formation, the tide having left a hollow in the sand filled with water. But ten yards farther on, I found another such map, and ten yards farther on, another, and another, and another. I was not inclined to accept such a regular pattern as accidental. Next morning, I discovered the answer—a little, lonely Australian boy, on vacation by himself, digging out maps of Australia with his spade and filling them with his bucket. That made more sense than accidental chance."

There was a babble of comment, but P. T. Liu remained silent. After a long pause, he asked, "Would you say that chance is an impossible explanation of the order of the universe?"

"No," said the Chaplain. "You could always say mathematically, there is a remote chance! Better say: Blind chance as an explanation of order in the universe is repugnant to common sense."

Chapter 3

HOW MUCH
MUST AN ATHEIST KNOW?

"I have been having a bad time with atheists," said
Harry McClelland. "I tell them that the fool has
said in his heart, there is no God. But that seems to
be more convincing to Christians than to atheists."

Some convinced Christians nodded, but there
was a different reaction from several present who
fancied themselves as philosophers. One of the latter spoke up. "Well, Harry," said Bonelli. "They
have a case. Atheists have a case. You can't go
around calling them fools just because they don't
agree with you."

"It's not a matter of agreeing with me," retorted
McClelland. "It's what the Bible says."

"Yeah," said Adams. "You and the Bible."

"Easy, men, easy," said the Chaplain. "You won't
get very far that way. It reminds me of family discussions when my children were young. You know
how it is? My teenage daughter said, 'I tell you it

is!' My teenage son said, 'I tell you it's not!' My daughter replied, 'You know nothing!' My son replied, 'You know nothing!' My daughter commented, 'Listen to the copy cat!' My son repeated, 'Listen to the copy cat!' My daughter retorted, 'Oh, shut up!' My son retorted, 'You shut up!' I told them: 'Both of you, shut up!' "

There was a roar of merriment. When their laughter died down, the Chaplain looked slyly at some of his hearers.

"I have been guilty of the same kind of debate myself," he went on. "I was crossing the Pacific with eight thousand American soldiers bound for Guadalcanal and New Guinea. One night I became involved in an argument with an atheist from Brooklyn. I can stand atheists, and I can stand people from Brooklyn, but atheists from Brooklyn are harder to take!"

Everyone laughed, and the Chaplain went on: "I asked him, 'Do you believe the Bible?' He replied, 'The Bible is only a book!' 'It's an inspired book,' I said.

" 'That's what you say!' he retorted.

"I asked him, 'Well, then. Do you believe in Christ?' He replied, 'Christ is dead!'

" 'He rose again,' said I.

" 'That's just what you say!' said he. So I asked him: 'Do you believe in God?'

"He replied, 'No, I'm an atheist!'

" 'What do you believe?' I asked.

" 'I believe that religion is a racket,' said he.

" 'No, it's not!' said I.

" 'Yes, it is!' said he.

"So I told him, 'That's just what you say!' "

When their laughter died away, the Chaplain

said quietly, "We have a visitor today who has not been introduced. I wonder if Mr. Weber would introduce the gentleman beside him."

"I present," said Philip Weber, "a visitor from Texas, Mr. S. Houston MacNeill."

"Howdy, folks!" said the latter, graciously. "You all call me Sam!"

"I have had a few words with Mr. MacNeill," said the Chaplain. "He became an atheist in '59."

"I thought," said P. T. Liu, "that all Texans were Baptists. A Texan in Hong Kong told me that, but I suppose he was jesting."

"Oh, I'm a Baptist all right," said S. Houston MacNeill. "My folks were Baptists from away back. So I'm a Baptist atheist!"

There was suppressed laughter.

"You kiddin'?" asked Lt. Petersen. "Are you a member of a Baptist Church?"

"I became non-resident," said Sam. "I was baptized in a lil' old Baptist Church in the Big Bend country, but when I became a sophomore at college, I became an atheist."

"Now," said the Chaplain, "I'd been expecting some discussion of atheists and agnostics, so I welcome Mr. MacNeill's—Sam's—presence, so that we can ask him some questions."

The tall Texan bowed.

Harry McClelland stared at him. He did not appreciate a Texan Baptist becoming an atheist, but he put it down to his not being able to 'rightly divide' the Word of Truth.

Said the Chaplain, "Mr. Bonelli remarked that atheists had a case. I wonder if Mr. Bonelli would favor us with a definition of an atheist."

"An atheist," said Bonelli, "is a man who denies the existence of God."

"I accept that definition," said the Texan.

"What is the weakness," asked Helen Johnson, "of the argument of the atheist?"

"It is this," said the Chaplain. "To deny the existence of God, one would need to be assured that God had no place in or beyond the universe. What is the extent of your cosmic knowledge, Bonelli?"

"Not such a lot," countered Bonelli.

"How about you, MacNeill?" asked Adams.

"Quite a lot," said Sam, modestly.

Bonelli turned to look at him in amazement. The tall Texan was claiming too much.

"Einstein said," observed Bonelli, "that the scientists are on the fringe of knowledge. So I will admit that I'm on the fringe of the fringe."

Said the tall Texan, "I think that scientists are doing pretty well."

Philip Weber turned to Bonelli. "How much do you know?" he asked, briefly. "Ten percent?"

"How much what?"

"Knowledge."

"In relation to what?"

"Total knowledge. Ten percent?"

"Less than one percent," replied Bonelli. "I mean I know far less than one percent of possible knowledge."

"Oh, I wouldn't say that," said MacNeill.

"Is it possible," asked Weber, "that God could exist outside your realm of knowledge?"

He addressed Bonelli, but the Texan replied, "Well, there is so little outside that I could say that it isn't likely."

Silence fell on the group. They were utterly

dumfounded. Bonelli began to betray indications of impatience with Sam. Looking to Adams for support, he launched an attack. "Are you trying to tell us that you know such a lot that you know that God could not exist?"

"Let us say so," said the Texan, evenly.

"Well, then," retorted Bonelli. "If that's what is meant by claiming to be an atheist, I'm not an atheist. And I'll take back my words that there is a case for atheism."

His pulse-rate was rising rapidly.

"As I see it," he went on. "To be an atheist, you'd need to know everything. To know everything, you'd need to be God yourself. And I'm not prepared to make claims that big."

The Texan threw back his head and laughed.

"Shall I tell them, Phil?" he asked Weber. Weber nodded and the Texan went on, "Actually, I'm a member of the Hollywood Christian Group, and I'm working in television."

He grinned as he looked around the group. "True," he explained, "I became an atheist when I went to college, but I quit. I am back with the Southern Baptists."

"But you said—" protested Helen Johnson.

"Think carefully what I said," replied Sam. "Besides, I was putting on an act."

Philip Weber turned to the belligerent Bonelli. "I'm sorry, Pat," he said. "I put him up to it. I wanted you to see how shaky the argument for atheism really is."

Bonelli's pulse was slowing again. He made a quick recovery. His friend Adams took up the argument. "Let me ask you, Phil," he challenged Weber, "whether Santa Claus could exist outside your fraction of knowledge?"

"Well," replied Weber, while the others held their breath, "if you define Santa Claus as a heavily built man, living at the North Pole, driving a reindeer team over the rooftops, I'll give you a hundred and one scientific contradictions. There are no contradictions of God as defined—as an infinite spirit."

Chapter 4

OF WHAT
IS AN AGNOSTIC SURE?

A thin, ascetic-looking Indian was present in the next discussion, so the Chaplain waited for someone to introduce him. Petersen stood.

"On my way back from overseas, Chaplain," he said, "I met a graduate student from India, Sri Sri Ramakrishna from Hyderabad. I am sure we all welcome him to our class."

"I am indeed happy to visit you. I want to learn as much as possible about your country, and I am sure that you would enjoy visiting my country. I am a Hindu, but I greatly admire the Christian faith. I am sure that we have much in common."

"What is the significance of your double name, sir?" asked Helen Johnson.

"It is not really a double name," he explained. "Sri is a title of respect, like Mister or sir. It is also a given name. The British have their Earl Russell, and you have your Earl Warren. Could you imagine some Earl Earl Russell?"

"We shall call you Mr. Ramakrishna," said the Chaplain. "Now, shall we return to our little discussion of atheism and agnosticism?"

"Bonelli and our friend from Texas had a big joke," said Adams. "Eh, Bonelli?"

"Well," said he, "I'm glad it showed that I don't make impossible claims. I'm not an atheist. Maybe I'm an agnostic."

"What's the difference?" asked Cynthia.

"An agnostic," explained the Chaplain, "is one who does not know whether God exists or not. The word was coined by Thomas Huxley."

"Then I'm an agnostic too," said Adams.

"What kind of agnostic are you?" asked the Chaplain, mischievously.

"Are there different kinds?" asked Adams.

"There are two main kinds," was the reply. "There are ordinary agnostics, and there are ornery agnostics. The ordinary agnostic," the Chaplain went on, "simply says that he does not know. The ornery one says that he does not know and that you do not know and that nobody knows. If you say, David, that you know that I do not know, I must ask you how you know that I do not know."

"I'll quit right there," said Adams. "I do not know, speaking for myself, and for Bonelli."

"If you like," interrupted the tall Texan, "I'll claim that I know that you don't know, all for the sake of argument."

His offer was declined.

"You've done enough damage," said Bonelli. "And we admit that we do not know."

"Okay," commented Weber, "if you say that you

don't know, boys, okay, so you don't know. But some of us know."

"You mean you think you know," said Adams.

"Okay," replied Weber. "I'll debate that with you any day. Did you ever believe in God?"

"Sure," admitted Adams. "When I was a kid at school, I believed in God."

"Maybe you were right then," insisted Weber, "and wrong now. Why did you stop believing?"

"Because," protested Adams, "I am a lot smarter now than I was then . . ." and then he wished he had not phrased it thus.

"Ho, ho!" said Jack Petersen. "You mean that it is stupid to believe in God. I know a man and so do you and he has a couple of doctorates in philosophy from the best of schools, yet he still believes in God more firmly than ever."

David Adams looked hurt.

"I'm sorry, Dave," said Petersen, sincerely. "No reflection on your studies, I mean."

"That's all right, Jack," said Adams. "I asked for it. You win. There are lots of smarter men than I ever hope to be who believe in God. But," he said, "there are brilliant men also who do not believe. Bertrand Russell, Julian Huxley!"

"These brilliant men," said Phil Weber, "are brilliant in fields of specialization. They do not need to be brilliant to say 'I do not know.' I am telling you, you cannot be brilliant in the field of not-knowing-ness, which word is Anglo-Saxon for agnosticism."

There came the inevitable question.

"What is the weakness," asked Helen Johnson, "of the argument of the agnostic?"

"The weakness," replied Weber, "is that it is wrong to assume that an agnostic may speak with authority upon something he admits that he does not know."

"I want to know," said Adams, "is it possible to prove the existence of God by reason?"

"Let us recapitulate," said the Chaplain. "If scientific proof is meant, the answer is no. But it is certain that faith in God is quite reasonable.

"Years ago, I had a debate with the president of a national Rationalist Society. It was held in a Town Hall, and its chairman was the neutral president of the Rotary Club, whose guest I had been. In the vestry, before the debate began, the chairman asked us whether we wished to take a vote at the end of the session. We both said no. 'But, as chairman of the debate,' he said, 'I am going to be asked the question, Who won?' We still felt that voting would not help much.

"'Then I have a suggestion,' said the chairman. 'You, Mr. Principal,' he told my opponent, 'are challenging our guest,' he nodded to me, 'on his statement at Rotary that faith in God is quite reasonable. To win the debate, you must show that what he says is unreasonable, or that what you say is more reasonable. Otherwise, you will leave his claim that faith is quite reasonable unrefuted, and you will be the loser.' He was!"

Chapter 5

WAS GOD
IN THE BEGINNING?

"**O**kay, Chaplain," said McClelland. "You do not need to prove the existence of God to me, but I won't object if you show how reasonable it is. Can faith in God be proved by a single argument?"

The Chaplain answered carefully, "I do not believe that faith in God is founded upon reason. The foundation of our faith is divine revelation.

"It is better to say that there are three main arguments for the existence of God which, taken together, show that faith in God is reasonable. These arguments are not to be taken as foundations, but rather as buttresses; not as proofs, but tests of a divine revelation rather than of an hypothesis. Of course, one test sometimes convinces an individual. And there are others to consider beside these three. I once met a university professor who told me that he gave up his atheism and believed in God through his realization of the prevalence of beauty in nature, which he could not otherwise explain."

P. T. Liu asked the Chaplain to name his three main tests, which he did, thus: "The theological explanation of the origin of the universe—cosmology; the theological explanation of the order in nature—teleology, and the theological explanation of morals in man—anthropology. Add the weight of reason to that of intuition and revelation and experience of God."

"What did you say?" asked Cynthia Moore. "Cosmology? and teleology? and anthropology? I am getting out of my depth."

"What is the proposition concerning the origin of the universe?" asked Helen Johnson. "Cosmology?"

"Let me answer," said Philip Weber. "It's this. Everything owes its existence to a producing cause of some sort. The universe as we know it owes its existence to some ultimate Cause which must be greater than what that Cause produced."

"But," protested Adams, "that does not mean that the ultimate Cause is the God of the Bible."

"The Bible says so," answered McClelland, forcefully. "And I believe it."

"I know you do, Harry," said the Chaplain. "But some doubters don't. So let us see whether the others are prepared to consider an ultimate Cause, leaving the character and nature of that Cause till later."

There was a chorus of agreement, so the next question was addressed to P. T. Liu and another foreign student who had been introduced as Nils Andersson from Lund in Sweden.

"Are scientists agreed that the universe had a beginning?"

The Swede replied in careful English. "Most scientists are agreed that the universe had a beginning and that it will come to an end, and this is in keeping with the law of entropy—"

"The law of what?" asked Helen Johnson.

"The law of entropy," repeated Weber, "the second law of thermodynamics that teaches the inevitable dissipation of all energy—"

"What big words!" exclaimed Helen.

Andersson hesitated.

"Please, Chaplain," protested Cynthia Moore. "Get these engineers and scientists to explain. They don't understand words we use in knitting!"

"Well," said the Chaplain. "Did you learn the first law of thermodynamics?"

"No," replied the girls together, while the philosophers, Bonelli and Adams, listened as well.

"The first law of thermodynamics," explained P. T. Liu, "is the principle of the conservation of energy."

The faces of the girls remained blank.

"That means," he continued, struggling for non-technical words, "that in a closed system, you don't get anything out that you don't put in."

"But isn't there a perpetual motion machine?" asked Harry McClelland.

"No," replied the Chinese. "There are some devices with very little friction, but even these need to use the energy of sunlight to run."

"That brings us," said Andersson, "to the second law of thermodynamics. The second law of thermodynamics teaches that energy is always breaking down into non-recoverable forms."

31

Lt. Petersen interrupted with a laugh. "If these girls understand gambling," he said, "maybe they'll get the idea that in the first law you don't get something for nothing, and in the second, you don't even break even."

"Look," added Weber, noting their difficulty. "The sun is a big furnace, but it is burning down, and if nothing interferes, it will burn out."

"Or take a pack of cards," explained Petersen. "Once you shuffle a deck of cards, you lose the order arranged by the manufacturer. The chance of getting that order back by shuffling is—someone say it for me—infinitesimal. You cannot unscramble an egg."

"Good illustration," commented Liu, "when one considers that the spread of heat is like the shuffling of cards. It is something that nature cannot reverse. The latest word is that the increase of entropy is not a fluctuation; in other words, the universe has always been running down."

At this point, the Chaplain intervened. "Is the law of entropy," he asked, "admitted as an argument for creation by scientists?"

"I think," said Andersson in his accented phrases, "that some do not admit it in this way on the grounds that the law applies to observable local heat systems, but cannot be demonstrated as applying to the universe beyond observation."

"A few scientists teach," conceded Weber, "that matter is being created in outer reaches of space, but this is a pure speculation which has not been at all demonstrated. In fact, the weight of evidence is against it. Look up the latest article in the *Encyclopaedia Britannica*."

"Let's summarize," added P. T. Liu. "This law of

entropy has greater acceptance among scientists than the familiar law of gravitation."

"Well, that's something," said Adams.

"Are we ready to proceed?" asked Weber.

"When do scientists say our world began?" asked the Chaplain.

"About five billion years ago," replied Liu.

"I don't believe it," said McClelland.

"What I don't understand," commented Helen Johnson, "is how they arrive at such a date, just like that!"

"I don't believe it," repeated McClelland, but no one asked him why, knowing his answer.

Said Nils Andersson, "Scientists have various ways of estimating the age of the earth, and of checking it."

"Tell us . . ." urged Cynthia Moore.

"The age of the oldest rock . . ." he began.

". . . the age of meteorites," Liu continued.

". . . the radio-activity of uranium isotopes," added Andersson.

". . . the distance of the moon," added Weber.

". . . the speed and distance of the galaxies," suggested Petersen.

". . . and other scientific calculations," said Andersson. "They all suggest an age of several billion years or so."

"I hear you talking," said McClelland. "But it does not convince me."

"Oh, listen, Harry," said Petersen, quietly. "You were an electrician before you started at Bible Institute. How would you like it if Cynthia here started to pooh-pooh what you learned about electricity? Scientists are not fools."

"I know what's bothering Harry," said Weber.

"So I'll ask the appropriate question: Does not the scientific estimate of several billion years as the age of our world contradict the statements of the Bible?"

"Yes," said Adams, eagerly.

"No," replied Weber, firmly. "The biblical account of the genesis of things simply states that 'In the beginning, God created the heaven and the earth . . .' with no date given for creation."

"Where does the date 4004 B.C. come from?" asked Bonelli, curiously.

"It is not in the Bible text," asserted Weber.

Bonelli appealed to the Chaplain, who nodded in support of Weber.

"Okay, okay," said Bonelli. "Your argument is that the universe owes its existence to some ultimate Cause which must be greater than what that Cause produced. It has not made me accept Christianity, but I'll grant that it is reasonable."

"Let's not go too fast," said the Chaplain. "Does therefore the argument from the origin of the universe prove conclusively the existence of God?"

He answered his own question.

"The theological explanation of the origin of the universe, cosmology, does not prove the existence of God but rather shows that it is reasonable to conclude that an infinitely great Cause is responsible for the beginning of the universe, confirming a truth already known by insight."

Chapter 6

DOES DESIGN
REQUIRE A DESIGNER?

"**C**haplain," said Cynthia Moore, "I would like to present Mr. Michael Stratton-Smith of Oxford University, a Commonwealth scholarship exchange student."

"How do you do!" said the Englishman, rising.

"Your college at Oxford?" asked the Chaplain.

"Balliol, sir!"

"How's the traffic at Carfax?"

"Ghastly, sir," replied the other.

"It was bad enough in the late 'forties," said the Chaplain. "Welcome to our group. What do you want us to call you?"

Both men were thinking of the double-barrelled name when the visitor replied, "My friends call me Michael, sir."

"Howdy, Mike!" called MacNeill with a wave of welcome. "Call me Sam."

"Thank you," said Stratton-Smith, an almost imperceptible moment later adding, "Sam."

"Michael," began the Chaplain, "already we have discussed the cosmological significance of the existence of God. Today we intend to discuss the teleological. The term is familiar to you?"

"Oh yes, sir!" replied the Englishman. "The word comes from the Greek *teleos*, and may be described popularly as an explanation of order."

"From a design to a designer?" asked Weber.

"Not properly," replied Michael. "Rather that the order and utility pervading a system imply intelligence and purpose, a teleology from utility to purpose and a eutaxiology from order to intelligence."

Cynthia Moore regarded her special guest with starry eyes, although she understood very little of what he said.

"What are you reading at Oxford?" asked the Chaplain. "Philosophy?"

"I hope to enter Foreign Service, sir," said Michael. "Philosophy is just a hobby."

"Thank you, Michael," said the Chaplain, in an effort to simplify the conversation for the others, asking, "What is the theological explanation of order in nature?"

"Let us put it this way," explained Weber. "That our universe is orderly is accepted by scientists and laymen alike, for all scientific investigations and experiments are based upon the orderliness of the universe."

"Are you sure of that, Phil?" asked Adams. "I mean, isn't there a lot of chaos in the cosmos? The molecules of gases in this room are just now bombarding each other in every which way. You couldn't call that order!"

"It has purpose," replied Weber. "If it were not for the diffusion of gases, life would be utterly impossible for humans."

"It has order, too," interrupted Andersson. "Scientists have discovered a pattern in it."

"The best explanation of the order that pervades the universe is," Weber continued, "an Intelligence of a greater magnitude. And as everything has its use, there must be purpose in it all."

"When our troops," said the Chaplain, "pulled out of Sansapor in what is now called Irian, they left behind a jeep. A Papuan came down the trail, preceded by his wife . . ."

Lt. Petersen interrupted. "I thought those guys always walked in front, with their wives trailing a respectful distance behind their lord and master."

"In peacetime, yes," said the Chaplain. "In wartime there was always a danger of landmines, so the lady walked in front . . . They discovered an abandoned jeep. They not only had never before seen a jeep, they had never seen a wheelbarrow. The woman asked, 'What is this?'

" 'I do not know,' he replied.

" 'What is it called?'

" 'I do not know.'

" 'What does it do?'

" 'I do not know.'

" 'Where did it come from?'

" 'I do not know.' He recognized the seat, so he sat on it. He turned the steering wheel; he blew the horn; he pulled on the brakes; he let them off again; he changed gears; he opened a glove compartment; but he understood nothing of what he was doing. He happened to touch the self-starter button. The jeep had been left in gear, so it rocked him. That

37

did not make much sense. He examined a few other devices, then touched the self-starter button again. It rocked him a second time. The third time he tried it, he happened to have his foot heavily on the clutch pedal, so the engine started up in front. He had never heard an engine running before. It sounded like a big cat purring. So he thought he would get out and run around to the front to see what was making the noise. When he did so, the engine stalled. He got back in again. He tried to start the motor again. It just rocked him. Then he remembered to put his foot down heavily on the clutch pedal.

"He had enough gumption to know that the pedal had something to do with the engine stalling, so he decided to let his foot off that clutch pedal slowly enough to give him time to run around to the front to see what was making the noise. As he did so, the whole jeep moved forward with him. He was driving—very much against his will. He dived out of the vehicle, and did not return for half an hour. When he did return, he rediscovered that he could drive. So he drove it across the clearing until he got stuck.

"His wife asked him again, 'What is this?'

" 'I do not know,' he replied.

" 'What is it called?'

" 'I do not know.'

" 'What does it do?'

" 'It goes by itself.'

" 'Where did it come from?'

" 'I do not know. But whoever made this thing must be a lot more intelligent than I am.' There are weaknesses in that illustration," said the Chaplain, "but it serves to illustrate the teleological argument."

There had been much merriment enjoyed as the story was told, then questions followed.

"Do not some philosophers say," asked Liu, "that God is nothing more than an idea in the mind of man?"

Michael Stratton-Smith replied, "Before man appeared, order in the universe had arisen, and if catastrophe destroyed man, order in nature would continue, so this notion leaves untouched the problem of accounting for order apart from man."

"On Morotai," said the Chaplain, "my tent-mate was a noted obstetrician from Philadelphia. We kept our minds off the air-raids at night by discussing in a foxhole the problems of politics, science, philosophy and religion. One night, the medical officer said to me:

" 'Now listen, Chaplain! God is nothing more than an idea in people's minds. If you were to talk to a Solomon Islander and ask him about God, he says that the thunder is God. But go to India and talk to an Indian peasant—he can explain the thunder, yet when an epidemic breaks out, he rushes to burn incense in his temple to gods. Travel down to Australia and you find an educated Australian who explains thunder and epidemics yet uses the term God to cover up what he cannot understand. What I am trying to say is that the farther we push back the frontiers of ignorance, the less we need an idea of God. God exists only in people's minds.'

"I told the medical officer that I wanted to take up the analogy that he had just given. Supposing one talked to a Solomon Islander and asked him, 'Have you ever heard of King George?' He would reply, 'Yes, me British subject, me belong King.' I would say, 'How do you know that there is such a person as King George?' The simple islander would reply, 'Me British subject. Me belong King.'

"When I ask him what he thinks King George is like, he answers in his own terms, remembering that a village chief has four wives, an island chief forty wives, so he suggests that King George is a very big chief with four thousand wives!"

"I say," interrupted Stratton-Smith. "Very primitive idea of constitutional monarchy!"

"Travel," said the Chaplain, "to India from the Solomon Islands and ask an Indian peasant what he thinks King George is like. He thinks in terms of a local rajah or a neighboring maharajah and says that King George is Imperial Raj.

"Down in Australia, an Australian would tell us that we do not understand monarchy. The King does not rule; he reigns, as the symbol of the Commonwealth. In London, you meet someone who attended Cambridge University with Prince Albert when he was Duke of York. You meet a little Princess who speaks of him as 'Daddy.' You talk to an American tourist who tells you that it is all right for the Limeys to have a King but that nobody needs one in America. You talk to a Russian who tells you that the Communists, when they take over, will destroy the King as a symbol of the capitalist system.

"Seven different ideas of King George but they do not change the character of King George, if he as a person existed. There may be a thousand and one ideas of God, but they do not change the character of God, granted his existence."

"Do not some philosophers assert," asked Pat

Bonelli, "that out of a purposeless universe real purpose arose in man?"

"That does not make sense," said Weber. "That any purpose in the universe has arisen from a purposeless universe does not make any sense. Who has the right to say that the universe is purposeless? I have heard a brilliant lecturer make this very proposition, but it does not jive."

"Even I can see that," said Cynthia Moore. "In every lesser manifestation of order observed, whether a spider's web or a lady's watch, the human mind looks for a purposeful intelligence—isn't that so?"

"I would say so too," commented Petersen. "The greater the order and purpose, the greater the need for a purposeful Intelligence to explain its existence. No, I have heard some clever men argue against teleology, but their arguments are feeble."

"Does, therefore," asked Pat Bonelli finally, "does the theological explanation of order in nature prove conclusively the existence of God?"

"The theological explanation of order in nature," said the Chaplain, "or teleology, does not prove the existence of God but rather shows that it is reasonable to conclude that a purposeful Intelligence is responsible for the order and the utility in nature, confirming a truth already known by insight."

Chapter 7

DOES MAN REQUIRE A GOD?

"We seem to be growing in numbers," said the Chaplain. "Today we welcome Mr. Rafferty Jones, who has just returned from Peace Corps service in an African republic."

The class turned its gaze upon a well-built American Negro, who acknowledged the greeting pleasantly and easily.

"I am very glad to be here," he said.

There was a pause, then Lt. Petersen hastened to ask, "Are you any relation of the man who ran the mile for Northwestern University?"

Jones smiled whimsically. "I guess," he replied, "the fellow who did is a younger brother of my older brother."

Petersen reached across to shake hands. "I'm an Evanston man myself," he explained warmly, adding, "This fellow's a great guy."

"What is our topic for today?" asked Bonelli.

The group checked memory and notes.

"What is the theological explanation of morality in man?" asked McClelland, reading his notes.

"May I reply, sir?" asked Stratton-Smith. "It is generally agreed that man is a moral, as well as an intellectual being. Some deny moral standards, but . . ."

"Excuse me, Michael," interrupted Adams. "I don't know anyone who denies moral standards but I know those who say that such standards are neither absolute nor universal."

"What do you mean?" asked Helen Johnson.

"For instance," replied Adams, "what seems wrong in one society of people is not wrong in another. I mean, in this country we insist upon monogamy and penalize polygamists. But in the Moslem countries, a man may have four wives. Who's to say that we are right and they wrong?"

"They have a point," said Cynthia Moore. "I mean, with all the girls there are around, maybe there ought to be another system here too."

There was a murmur of merriment.

"Cynthia!" said Houston MacNeill. "Whattya mean? There are a hundred and one boys born for every ninety-nine girls!"

"Yes," said Cynthia defiantly. "What happens to them all?"

"The death rate for males," explained Liu, "is slightly higher for the first year, after which the sexes are equal. Then other hazards, such as war, reduce the number of men."

"The figure for this country is ninety-six or so men for a hundred women," added Petersen, briefly. "That's close enough."

"Have you anything to add to this?" said the

Chaplain to Rafferty Jones, hoping to bring him into the conversation again.

"I have worked in Africa," replied Jones. "I had the same idea as Mr. Adams when I went, but I changed. First of all, the Prophet Mahomet did not say that a man must have four wives. He said that a man might have four wives if he could support them. In the second place, many of the Islamic countries upon gaining independence are abolishing polygamy in favor of monogamy."

"Why?" asked Adams in a surprised voice.

"You'd really have to live there to understand. In the old days, if a man got tired of his wife and wanted to trade her in for a later model, all he needed to do was to clap his hands and say in the presence of witnesses, 'I divorce thee.' The wife had neither family nor property rights. She was unable to claim the furniture or the children."

"What about the Mormons?" asked Adams.

"That is another story," replied Petersen. "One of the reasons given for polygamy is the outnumbering of men by women in certain times with the need of repopulation. But in the very next generation, the numbers of each sex are equalized. That would apply to Germany after World War II. Polygamy could not be a universal rule, that's certain."

"But it would be justified if . . ." said Adams.

"Look, man," McClelland retorted. "Suppose a hundred fellows from Harvard and a hundred girls from Radcliffe should decide to colonize the Galapagos Island. Suppose the campus bully goes along and decides to annex four blondes, three brunettes and three redheads." There was a burst of laughter. "What do you think will happen? Ninety-nine men will be left with the ninety available girls! Suppose ten men decide to take the Moslem quota of four wives each. That leaves fifty girls for eighty fellows! How stupid could we get?"

"In that connection," said the Chaplain, "I once visited Pitcairn Island in the far-off Pacific. I met the descendants of Fletcher Christian and the mutineers of the Bounty. The mutineers and several Tahitian men with a lesser number of Tahitian women settled the island. Quarreling and murder followed disputes about the women, until only one man, John Adams, survived, with a flock of Tahitian women and Anglo-Polynesian children. Adams saw the extinction of the colony unless something was done. So he taught the ten commandments from the Bible. The sexes were equalized among the surviving children, and the Pitcairn Islanders became one of the most moral communities in the world. Polygamy would have destroyed them."

"In Hollywood," called Rafferty Jones, "they have a system called progressive monogamy—one woman at a time!"

"Or one man at a time," added Weber.

"And look what misery it causes," commented McClelland. "Legalized prostitution, I say!"

"Not quite," interjected Adams.

"No, not quite," said McClelland bitterly. "I pity all the poor kids with their daddys and ex-daddys and ex-ex- and ex-ex-ex-daddys."

"Well," said Petersen. "Not very many can afford it. Some dumb guys are broke because of it."

"How did we get started on this?" asked Helen Johnson. "How did we get off the subject?"

"We are not really off the subject," replied Philip Weber. "The point is that there exists a universal

46

morality. Does this apply to the other points of the Ten Commandments?"

"Sure," said Harry McClelland. "Thou shalt not steal . . ."

"But aren't there peoples who don't worry at all about stealing?" asked Bonelli.

"In New Guinea," replied Petersen, "I met savages who didn't mind stealing, but they hated like mad to be robbed."

"Why pick on the poor savages?" retorted Adams. "There are people in this country who would rob you blind."

"Sure," said McClelland, "but we can stand only so many of them. If they get too numerous, it would be impossible to carry on business."

"Okay," said Bonelli, "nobody's defending stealing. What next?"

"The same thing goes for lying," said Weber. "People lie, but nobody wants to be deceived."

"How about murder?"

"That's a universal law, too, even though not everyone obeys it."

Cynthia Moore turned to Michael Stratton-Smith and Nils Andersson and asked, "What do you foreigners think of life in the United States, judging from our television? Or from our movies?"

Michael Stratton-Smith was startled to hear himself described as a foreigner, so he hesitated while the Swede answered evenly, "Well, sometimes we wonder."

Said the Chaplain, "I once preached in a town in the wildest part of Latin America, where there was a murder a day. The only cure was sending for police from better ordered communities, or estab-

47

lishing a vigilante committee as in the Wild West here."

"Okay," said Adams. "Nobody's in favor of stealing or lying or killing. But aren't modern ideas of contraception changing the old morality about pre-marital and extra-marital sex?"

"That does not make it right," retorted the aroused Harry McClelland. "What is the real purpose of sex? Procreation. No, don't interrupt me! I recognize companionship but procreation takes precedence. Promiscuity with or without contraception leads to venereal disease, abortion and more misery for children. Statistics prove that statement."

Adams shrugged his shoulders.

"Statistics prove the case, Dave," said Jack Petersen, quietly. "Come along now. You are no more in favor of adultery and fornication than you are in favor of stealing and killing. You want a girl just like the girl that married dear old Dad. You have just been arguing."

"Okay, okay," said Adams. "But someone tell me why it is that most college students and guys in military service are sort of concerned about this subject?"

"I suppose," said Petersen, "it's the fact that the sex urge develops at fifteen but most fellows for educational and economic reasons are not married until twenty-five or so. It's a fact that middle-aged men are leery of some guys coming to court their daughters."

There was a pause. Some present were a bit reluctant to continue the discussion lest it seem that they were preoccupied with the subject. The Chaplain saw now an opportunity to ask Michael Stratton-Smith to return to his long-forgotten statement of morality in man.

"It is generally agreed that man is a moral as well as an intellectual being," he began again. "We can sum it up this way. Some deny moral standards; but although some steal, none enjoy being robbed; though some lie, none enjoy being deceived; though some murder, none enjoy being murdered.

"The explanation of morality in man is this. The moral like the intellectual nature of man has for its author a moral and intellectual Being, for mere matter cannot account for man's intellect and morality."

"Is there any other evidence existing in man," asked P. T. Liu, "to suggest that his nature must be derived from another and greater Being?"

"Yes, certainly," said Stratton-Smith quickly. "Conscience and emotion to some degree exist in all men. Any man who violates his conscience is oppressed by feelings of guilt that stem from a higher moral law not self-imposed, for man's conscience may act as a prosecuting attorney, while man's emotions, being imperfect, seek an emotional ideal in the perfect emotion of God."

This was received without comment. They were all becoming a little tired, mentally. So when the Chaplain suggested that the class could discuss the nature of man more fully another time, P. T. Liu posed the summarizing question:

"Does therefore the theological explanation of morals in man conclusively prove the existence of God?"

The Chaplain replied, "The theological explanation of morals in man," he said, "or anthropology,

49

does not prove the existence of God but rather shows that it is reasonable to conclude that an infinitely great intellectual and moral Being has endowed all men with such a nature, confirming a truth already known by insight."

Chapter 8

IS FAITH IN GOD REASONABLE?

"**C**haplain," said Rafferty Jones, "I brought an African student, Mr. Zefani Mhlongwa."

"Sa' Bona," said the Chaplain.

The visitor's dark lips parted in a smile. "You speak Zulu, Umfundis?"

"No, but I have traveled in Zululand and in Swaziland and farther south. With your name, I take it that you are from near Pondoland?"

"Yes," said the African, delightedly. "I was helping at a mission station in Swaziland—that's how I was able to come out on scholarship, but I was born in the Umzimkulu valley."

"I have been trying," added Rafferty Jones, "to give Zefani a summary of our discussions. What are the chief contributions of the three applications of the existence of God—let me see if I can remember them—to the origin of the universe, to the order in nature, and to morals in man?"

"Let me recapitulate," replied the Chaplain. "The cosmological explanation stresses the idea of a creative Power; the teleological explanation stresses the idea of a planning Intelligence, and the anthropological explanation stresses the idea of a personal Holiness, the very attributes of the God revealed in Scripture."

"If these considerations of God are not conclusive arguments or proofs," asked Rafferty Jones, "how then do we learn the reality of God?"

"That's a good question," said the Chaplain. "These considerations serve to show that faith in God is not unreasonable, that indeed it is more reasonable than the alternatives."

"The Bible says," stated Harry McClelland, "it is by faith that we understand that the worlds were created, beautifully coordinated, and now exist at God's command; so the things that we see did not develop out of mere matter."

"What are you reading from?" asked Weber.

"Williams' Translation," said McClelland, "Hebrews chapter eleven, verse three."

"That's all very well, Harry," said Bonelli. "Is it not disappointing to ask us to accept the fact of God's existence by faith when an astronomer presents his facts confirmed by telescope and a biologist his facts confirmed by microscope?"

"We each accept the fact," replied Petersen, "of the reality of our own existence by faith. Think it through! Faith is not mere credulity or superstition, which run contrary to reason."

"Faith is an insight," repeated the Chaplain, "whereby we grasp the 'proof of the reality of the things we cannot see.' That's also from the Williams' Translation, Hebrews eleven, one."

"But can faith be considered as a reliable faculty?" asked Bonelli.

"Faith is not only reliable, but imperative," replied the Chaplain. "A student once asked me: 'Why is it that you religious people cannot prove anything? A biologist can take you to his microscope, and an astronomer to his telescope, but you religious people are always talking about taking things by faith. Aren't you trying to put one over on us?'

"'Man,' said I, 'can't you see that true faith is a kind of eyesight? It is a spiritual perception of the reality of the unseen.'

"Just suppose for a moment that everyone in this class were blind from birth, and I am asked by its professor to deliver a lecture upon color. I begin by saying, 'Ladies and gentlemen, color is a manifestation of light.' Up goes a hand, with a question.

"'Sir, before we go further, what is light?'

"'Don't you know what light is?' I ask. 'Light is a kind of radiation, part of the spectrum of energy. You know what heat is? Well, just as heat radiates warmth, light makes things visible.'

"Another hand is raised. 'What is visible?'

"So I explain that visible means 'able to be seen,' but this means nothing to my audience. 'If light,' I continue, 'strikes a prism of glass, it is broken up into a spectrum of color on the wall, like a rainbow.'

"Up goes another hand. 'Sir, what is a rainbow?'

"I explain that a rainbow is caused by the refraction of the sun's rays in a rain cloud, that a rainbow is red and blue and green. They ask me to explain what green looks like . . . and I can only tell them that it is a secondary color, a mixture of yellow and blue. And they ask me what blue looks like, and

I'm stymied. I can only say that the essential characteristic of blue is its bluishness. Then a student inquires, 'Is color perception some kind of feeling?'

"What can I say? Of course, it is a feeling. Just as a nerve in the leg conveys a sensation of pain to the brain, the optic nerve conveys a sensation of color. Then he asks, 'Is it possible to describe color in scientific terms without referring to this feeling of color?'

"So I explain that a Swedish scientist named Angstrom measured the wavelength of light. Red is seven thousand Angstrom units, and blue is four thousand eight hundred. Do you think for a moment that all those students, blind from birth, would nod their heads in appreciation of the exact language of science? A poor old washerwoman with the blessing of eyesight knows more about color than a blind mathematician. And one with the perception of faith in God knows more about the 'why' of the universe than the most brilliant unbeliever.

"It may be objected that the blind have ways of realizing that the seeing possess a faculty which they do not share, such as stumbling over a chair about which the seeing friend warned them. Exactly, and when the spiritually blind realize that believers possess a faculty of spiritual sight, their eyes are opened—and that is the difference."

P. T. Liu had remained quiet until this point. "Is it not a question of semantics?" he asked.

"The meaning of words," whispered Bonelli to the girls.

"What does it mean to know?" Liu went on. "I know that oxygen constitutes about twenty-one percent of the atmosphere. How do I know? I have demonstrated it in the laboratory. Would you say

54

that you know God like that? Could you demonstrate the existence of God?"

His question was addressed to the group, but his eyes were turned to the Chaplain.

"How would you demonstrate?" replied he. "We have already discussed the inability of the scientist to establish spiritual truth. But we can not rule out spiritual evidence. And it would be a bold man to deny all the weight of accumulated evidence on that subject."

"Spiritual things," offered McClelland, "are spiritually discerned. That's what the Bible says. 'It is by faith that we understand that the world was framed by the word of God.'"

"And that," added Michael Stratton-Smith, "does not mean that it is a choice between being an intellectual and a believer."

"Many people," added the Chaplain, "accept a fallacy without examination. It is certainly a fallacy to assume that an agnostic may speak out with authority upon something he admits that he does not know."

The Chaplain smiled, then added a story. "It reminds me of the fellow in Los Angeles who was writing his doctor of philosophy thesis on alcoholism. To earn his degree, he knew it would be necessary to add a contribution to the field of knowledge. But what new thing could he hope to discover? He hit upon the idea that if he could discover the common denominator in all experiences of drunkenness, that common denominator might prove to be the actual cause of alcoholism.

"The candidate found an old fellow on Skid Row who offered to do the necessary research for him for nothing but the raw materials. On Monday, the old fellow got drunk with whiskey and soda; on Tuesday, he got drunk with brandy and soda; on Wednesday, he got drunk with rum and soda; on Thursday, he got drunk with gin and soda; and on Friday, he got drunk with vodka and soda. So the candidate asked himself: 'What makes him get drunk? It must be the common denominator. It must be the soda.'"

The laughter was loud and long.

Zefani Mhlongwa approached the Chaplain at the conclusion of the discussion, "Umfundis," he said. "This philosophy is new to me, but we Bantu like a good story. Yah! I will come again."

Chapter 9

WHERE DOES
KNOWLEDGE START?

"What I don't understand is this," said David Adams. "Why should we be so concerned about the existence of God? It is an interesting question, but the world keeps rolling for those who believe in God as well as those who don't."

Some of the class regarded him in amazement. It was Petersen who answered.

"Look, Dave," said he. "I love my neighbors but I put my love for my family above that. I love my family, but I put my country before that—in times of emergency. I love my country, but if I had to choose—which God forbid—I would put my God before country and family and neighbors. But that does not make me a poor neighbor or a poor head of the house or a poor patriot. Rather, and I think that history will bear me out, faith in God makes me a better citizen, a better man."

"The question is," said Rafferty Jones, "Is therefore knowledge of God to be considered of first importance, not as a philosophical hobby?"

"If there is an Almighty God," replied Weber, "from whom the whole universe and all human life is derived, then a vital relationship with God is the most important of all life's relationships, and ascertaining the will of God is life's most worthy objective."

"At Oxford University," said Stratton-Smith, "the Doctors of Divinity still head the academic processions, for theology is the queen of science. The fear of the Lord is the beginning of wisdom."

"Is it not enough just to know the right and to act upon it, to live a decent life without bothering about the supernatural?" asked Bonelli.

Adams added, "Socrates said that men will do the right if they only know the right."

"Don't kid yourself," retorted Petersen. "If that were so, our educational system would have reduced crime to a minimum, whereas we are experiencing a moral breakdown."

"Ancient history and modern records," said the Chaplain, "show that knowing the right does not always result in doing the right."

"Look at Germany and Japan before the war," observed MacNeill. "One was the most literate country in Europe and the other most literate country in Asia. They drenched both continents in blood."

"Hold on," objected Adams. "We and our allies were not without fault, were we?"

"Exactly," said Stratton-Smith. "That's what we are saying. Before the war, we had a most extraordinary chap in Britain—Professor C. E. M. Joad, of the B.B.C. Brains Trust. He was the Professor of Philosophy at London University."

"Professor Joad was such a witty enemy of the Christian gospel," interrupted the Chaplain, "that, when I was there, a London rector of the Church of England preached a sermon on 'God, the Devil, and Professor C. E. M. Joad'!"

There was a burst of laughter.

"Professor Joad held," continued Michael, "that there was nothing wrong with human nature that a better education, better opportunity and better environment would not cure.

"Came the war. When Joad contemplated the misery of torment and destruction, he came to the conclusion that current events and history as well constitute a long record of man's inhumanity to man. He came to see that the theologians shared an insight not stressed by scientific philosophers—there is something wrong with human nature and it might be called original sin. From that premise, Joad proceeded to the need of salvation from sin, and from the Saviour to the God who sent him to atone for man. Joad had an intellectual conversion and so became a member of the Church of England.

"The better education, better opportunity and better environment," he concluded, "have not in modern times produced a better society, as the rising crime rate in affluent societies shows."

"Let me ask a question!" said McClelland. "If science can tell us nothing at all about God, how then are we to learn the necessary truths for right living, such as the forgiveness of sins, the regeneration of personality, the certainty of judgment and the hope of immortality?"

"Science is silent on these," said Petersen. "Since human insight and scientific reasoning tell us nothing about these important questions, we must depend upon God himself to reveal all the answers to us. Thus we need not only true insight and clear reasoning, but also revelation upon which to build experience."

P. T. Liu joined the conversation again, much to the satisfaction of all thoughtful hearers, even though his attitude was agnostic inquiry.

"From what sources," he asked, "does the Christian derive his knowledge of the origin of the universe of life and matter?"

It was the Chaplain who answered him. "Knowledge of the origin of the world around us is derived from the observation of God's work in science, as well as from the study of God's word in Scripture."

"And how do we gather such knowledge?"

"Scientific truth is accumulated by the scientific method, and scriptural truth is gleaned by careful study of the documents."

"But is there not an actual conflict between Scripture and science?" asked Bonelli.

"From the observations of science are derived theories," answered the Chaplain. "From the study of Scripture are derived interpretations. Generally, I would say, the conflict is between the theories of some scientists and the interpretations of some expositors rather than between the facts of science and the text of Scripture."

"I wish," said Cynthia Moore, "that somebody would give me an example. What theories? What interpretations?"

"Some people still believe in the flat earth theory . . ." began Philip Weber.

"You're kidding," said Rafferty Jones.

"No, I'm not," replied Weber. "There's an association somewhere in Missouri that teaches seriously that the earth is flat. And so does an organized denomination in Illinois! But their odd interpretation of certain poetic phrases in the Bible conflicts with established facts of science."

"How about an example of the opposite? Of a scientific theory contradicted by Scripture?"

"Well," intervened Michael Stratton-Smith, "it depends what you mean by scientific. The theory that life generated spontaneously is held by reputable scientists and it is denied by the Scripture. The Scripture teaches a process of development, but not spontaneous generation."

There was a moment's pause.

"I think," said Nils Andersson, in his careful Scandinavian-accented English, "that we must ask ourselves two questions: Are there limits to the scope of science and also limits to the purpose of Scripture?"

"Very well put!" commented Stratton-Smith. "Science is silent about spiritual things, for by the scientific method we are unable to discover anything about the basic spiritual fact of the universe, the existence of God."

"On the other hand," added Harry McClelland, "the purpose of Scripture is limited by statements therein to the teaching of doctrine, for reproof and correction, and for training in doing right."

"I would accept that," agreed Philip Weber, "though its many references to mundane matters are not unscientific."

"Do we need Scripture to help us in science?" asked Pat Bonelli.

"Well," replied Weber, "science omits from its consideration the ultimate spiritual truths. But," he added, "science is built up by the scientists, who as men need ultimate answers."

"Then why should we allow science to check Scripture interpretations?" asked McClelland.

"We rightly use the most recent conclusions of archaeology, botany, geography, history and zoology," said the Chaplain, "to substantiate biblical statements or re-interpret doubtful points.

"Some Christians betray reluctance only in recognizing the conclusions of geology and its related departments, not realizing that the clash which they resent is a clash of debatable theory versus doubtful interpretation."

On that note, the discussion concluded.

Chapter 10

WHAT'S THE CHOICE?

"**S**ir," said David Adams at the beginning of a session, "I have brought with me a geology student to join in the discussion, Mr. Charles R. Fitzgerald, formerly of Boston."

"And I have brought with me, Chaplain," said Pat Bonelli, "an anthropology student, Mr. Fritz Wagner, who was born in Hamburg."

The Chaplain smiled, thinking to himself that the two philosophers had gotten together to add variety to the company, seeing that their fellow-student Philip Weber was an avowed Christian.

"Welcome, gentlemen," said the Chaplain. "I see that we have an astronomer, a geologist and an anthropologist in our group, besides engineers and theologians and philosophers. This is fitting, seeing that we intend discussing the debatable question of Creation. Now, who has a question?"

Neither of the visitors spoke, and the Chaplain

was not surprised when Bonelli began: "Is there a conflict admitted between Scripture and science regarding the origin and development of the heavens and the earth?"

"Let me answer that," replied Philip Weber. "The conflict appears to be between debatable theories of some scientists and doubtful interpretations of some expositors rather than a conflict between the facts of science and the text of Scripture, between which there appears to be a very remarkable harmony."

David Adams waxed indignant. "You don't mean to tell me," he protested, "that you believe all that superstition in the first chapter of Genesis! Sir!"

"What superstition?" asked Weber, calmly.

"Why!" continued Adams. "It's no better than the myths and legends of the Babylonians, or the Egyptians, or the Aztecs, or the Japanese."

"Do you know what you are talking about?" asked Weber, a little more sharply.

"Well," said Pat Bonelli, supporting his old friend, "my professor called the Genesis story 'a flight of poetic fancy!'"

"Very well, then," retorted Weber, aroused. "Will either of you two gentlemen give us an outline of the Babylonian creation myth so that we can compare it with Genesis?"

There was a painful silence.

Then Fritz Wagner spoke. "The Babylonians," he began, "taught in their Epic of Creation that in the beginning there were two gods only, Apsu and Tiamat . . ."

"Tiamat was a female dragon," said Cynthia Moore abruptly.

"How do you know?" asked MacNeill.

"I read it somewhere," replied Cynthia, with a coy smile.

"That's right," said Wagner with a frown. "Apsu and Tiamat were in chaos, but from their union sprang all the gods of heaven and earth, who rebelled, and sought to create an orderly universe. The male god of chaos, Apsu, was defeated by the god Ea, who became the deity of water. But Tiamat, the female god of chaos, chased out Ea and Anu, the heaven god. Marduk, the son of Ea, was raised to first rank to battle with Tiamat and eleven monsters and her hosts and her husband. The eleven monsters he chained to the stars. He then defeated Tiamat herself and divided her body, making one half of it into the vault of heaven and the other half of it into the habitation of earth. Ea created man from the blood of the slain husband of the dragon. I cannot remember any more."

"Splendid synopsis," responded the Chaplain. "Now perhaps Mr. Wagner will give us a similar synopsis of Genesis."

To everyone's surprise, the visitor abruptly declined, asking to be excused. Neither Adams nor Bonelli was able to oblige.

"Well," said Bonelli, "it's a long time since I read it. But it's crazy."

"Harry," said the Chaplain, "lend Pat your Bible so that he can check. Phil, will you give us a synopsis of the story of Genesis."

"First of all," explained Weber, "Genesis says that in the beginning, God made the material universe, the heavens and the earth. At that time, the earth was dark and chaotic, presumably a dark nebula of sorts. In order, Genesis states that God caused light to radiate; that God made the celestial expanse; that he caused the land masses to separate from the oceans; that thereupon God commanded the earth to produce its self-propagating vegetation; that he instituted the days, seasons and years by means of celestial clocks; that he caused the oceans to produce living things, proceeding to birds of the air; that he caused the earth to produce all kinds of beasts, and finally made man to have dominion over all plants and animals. That's the story in a nutshell."

"Question," said Petersen. "Can the Genesis account of Creation be regarded as a flight of poetic fancy similar to and derived from other fanciful primitive creation stories of antiquity?"

"What about the other stories?" asked Helen Johnson. "The Egyptian and Aztec and so on?"

"Well, I say," said Michael Stratton-Smith, "the others are even more weird. The Babylon Epic of Creation is reckoned closest to Genesis. Between the fanciful creation stories of other ancient traditions and the Genesis account there is an absolute gulf, the latter being monotheistic and reasonable, the others polytheistic or pantheistic and fantastic, though sometimes these legends possess an element of truth derived from an earlier source, as in Babylonian legends."

"Any comment, gentlemen?" asked Weber.

There was a long pause before Adams spoke. "Well, Phil," he said, "the way you made it sound, you would think that you were quoting from the *Encyclopaedia Britannica* plus references to God. You had me stymied."

"But you had the actual text in front of you!"

"Yes," replied Bonelli. "And allowing for the quaint biblical language, what you said was in keeping with the text, with a few points I wish to have explained."

"Is the Genesis account of Creation," asked Nils Andersson, "to be regarded as history?"

"It is truth," replied Weber. "But if history be considered as an account of events compiled from the observations of human eyewitnesses, it seems obvious that the first thirty-four verses of Genesis did not arise from the accounts of human observers. That's certain."

"How do you classify these verses?"

"They must be treated as pictorial highlights revealed by God to some ancient patriarch and recorded by the great lawgiver, Moses, or his editorial secretary."

"What do you mean?" asked Helen Johnson. "Pictorial highlights? What do you mean?"

"Well," responded Rafferty Jones. "I saw in a national magazine a life-story of President Lincoln from old photographs. They were only flashes of truth, but they told the story."

Chapter 11

WHAT DOES THE BIBLE SAY?

"Why is such an important theme as Creation conveyed by pictorial highlights instead of some detailed scientific treatise?" asked P. T. Liu.

It was the Chaplain who replied, "The purpose of God seems not to have been to describe in detail the expansion of the material universe and the development of life on earth—things that a scientist could discover for himself, but rather to reveal God's part in creation, which no scientist could possibly discover. The use of paragraph-pictures seems the most suited to the purpose of reaching mankind in every stage of cultural development, from savage to savant.

"I remember teaching the Creation story to savage Papuans; it was not beyond them. Yet my professor of geology at Northwestern told me that he was amazed at the scientific accuracy of Genesis."

"But," protested Adams, "it says that the sun was created in the fourth day!"

"Excuse me," replied Weber. "It does not use the word 'create,' but uses instead the word 'made' which carries the meaning of 'made to function.' And that is what must have happened. The rocket probe showed Venus surrounded by dense clouds. The earth was so hidden once."

"Then the sun was made to appear?"

"So it would seem."

"Then from what point of view is the pictorial record of Creation given?" asked Petersen.

"If," explained Weber, "Genesis had used the jargon of twentieth-century astronomy, it would have been as incomprehensible as if it had been written in the language of angels. The Genesis account is given from a human and earth-centered point of view, not from an angelic or astronomical frame of context; otherwise the account would be incomprehensible to many generations and many conditions of men."

"In view of the date 4004 B.C.," asked Adams, "does Scripture set a date for the Creation?"

"That was answered before," replied Weber. "Scripture simply states that 'In the beginning God created the heaven and the earth, and the earth was without form and void, and darkness was on the face of the deep.' With such a simple paragraph-picture, science has no quarrel."

" 'In the beginning . . .' " prompted Adams.

"Let me quote the *Encyclopaedia Britannica*: Cosmogonists using the new values of measuring the distances between galaxies have obtained an estimated five billion years' total as the age of the universe, which is in perfect agreement with other astrophysical and geological calculations."

"'. . . God created . . .'" continued Bonelli.

"According to Enrico Fermi and others," said Weber, "the result of the super-thermonuclear explosion which produced the universe was the creation of matter ninety-nine percent hydrogen-helium and one percent slightly heavier matter. In this accepted theory, elements were formed during the first half-hour of the existence of the universe. That is not so staggering when one realizes that the creative period in a nuclear explosion is one microsecond compared to the months or years that atomic products linger."

"'. . . the heaven . . .'" prompted Fitzgerald.

Philip Weber continued: "Adapting Einstein's theory of relativity, the astronomer George Gamow suggested that light gas expanded throughout the universe, with no aggregation of matter for quarter of a billion years. These gas clouds formed cold proto-galaxies which account for our galaxies today.

"It is true that Fred Hoyle and others have propounded their theory of continuously created matter. All evidence noted in *Encyclopaedia Britannica* seems to contradict Hoyle's theory.

"Sir James Jeans suggested that gravity and radiation caused the condensation of the diffuse matter into stars, and Whipple that these stars by radiation helped to form new stars."

"'. . . and the earth . . .'" prompted Wagner.

"It was Immanuel Kant," said Weber, "who suggested that the planets had condensed from a solar nebula, a spinning disk. Maxwell showed that a spinning disk of uniform gravity would be broken up into a mass of materials rather than planets. So

71

Sir James Jeans and others mooted the collision theory—that some wandering star came too close to our sun and tore pieces off. Weizsacker disposed of this theory in 1944 by demolishing a wrong premise.

"Until World War II, it was generally believed that the sun and stars and other interstellar material was of the same gravity as the earth's. It was discovered that the terrestrial elements formed less than one percent of such matter and that hydrogen and helium accounted for ninety-nine percent. This forced a return to Kant's idea.

"It was Kuiper who refined the theory. He proposed that gravitation caused the formation of the proto-planets, which were formed largely of the lighter gases, but with some heavier dust. The lighter gas envelopes of the nearer planets were blown away by solar radiation, but left in the case of the farther-out planets."

And the earth was without form, and void; and darkness was upon the face of the deep (Genesis 1:2).

"An important point in Kuiper's theory," said Weber, "is that the formation of 'protoplanets' took place in darkness before the sun was sufficiently condensed to emit light. A dust cloud. We must insist that Genesis states in two verses a scientific, up-to-date cosmogony."

"Thank you," said the Chaplain, sincerely.

Chapter 12

HOW LONG
DID GOD CREATE?

"Chaplain," said P. T. Liu, "I would like to make a personal statement, if I may."

"Certainly," agreed the Chaplain.

"I would like to apologize for my attitude . . ."

"Apologize?" echoed the Chaplain. "My dear Mr. Liu, you have nothing to apologize for! You have been a model of courtesy and contribution. This class would be lost without you."

"Nevertheless," said the Chinese engineer, "I owe you all an apology. I have been getting a lot out of this class. It has satisfied my sense of fair play as well as curiosity. I must confess," he went on, "that I had a rather patronizing attitude towards Christianity, however. I was mildly in favor of it, as I am in favor of Santa Claus for children. Whatever good was in it, I thought must be in its kernel of moral teaching. But I thought that the faith was hopelessly unscientific. The discussions—and particularly what Mr. Weber said in the last discussion —have shaken my smug complacency. I realize that I have been despising a caricature of what Scripture teaches. I apologize."

"And I should apologize," said the Chaplain, "for the fact that you, an intelligent visitor from overseas, should suffer the misrepresentation of such a caricature without immediately hearing an academically respectable case for scriptural truth. I wish I could blame it all on the enemies of Christianity. I must blame a lot of it on the well-intentioned but thoughtless caricaturing of the truth by friends."

There was a pause, then Bonelli said, "That was a courageous thing to say, Peetee. I cannot apologize for my attitude, but I confess that the last class shook me up a bit, too. I have a question. Phil Weber made out a good case for scientific validity in the Genesis Creation story. If it were not all instantaneous creation, what other methods of creation are attributed to God by Scripture?"

Michael Stratton-Smith replied. "That God's work in creation," he explained, "is both direct and indirect is indicated by the use of Hebrew verbs translated 'create,' 'make' and 'form' as well as in such expressions as 'let there be ...', 'let the earth bring forth . . .' and 'let the waters bring forth.' Some scholars will dispute, for example, a distinction between 'create,' 'make' and 'form,' yet different verb roots are used—for a purpose, I think."

"What does Genesis say that God 'created'?" asked Rafferty Jones.

"The Genesis account states that God created the material universe," said Lt. Petersen, "and God created life in the oceans, and God created man in the spiritual image of God. The verse references

74

for those three citations are Genesis chapter one, verses one, twenty-one and twenty-seven."

"Isn't it interesting," commented P. T. Liu, "that those three creative acts coincide with the three scientific mysteries, the creation of matter and the appearance of life and the spirituality of man? I find this interesting. I am surprised in spite of myself."

"What does Scripture state that God made," asked Rafferty Jones, "or that God formed, or that God caused a natural agency to produce?"

All eyes turned to Philip Weber, but Cynthia Moore said quickly, "I made shorthand notes of Phil's synopsis. I thought it was so good. Let me read them in the order he quoted from Genesis:

"God caused light to radiate; then God made the celestial expanse; then he caused the land masses to separate from the oceans; and then God commanded the earth to produce its own self-propagating vegetation; then he instituted days, seasons, and years by means of celestial clocks; then he caused the oceans to produce life, fish and reptiles, then birds in the air; then he caused the earth to produce all kinds of beasts and finally made man to have dominion over all plants and animals."

"Okay," commented David Adams. "What about these days of Genesis?"

"Does Scripture teach that God accomplished all his creative work in six days of twenty-four hours, a total of a hundred and forty-four hours?" asked Helen Johnson.

Michael Stratton-Smith answered her. "There are many interpretations of the 'days.' The Hebrew word 'yom' is used in Scripture more than a hundred times to denote longer than a twelve or twenty-four hour day, being used for an age, a space, a time, a season, a life, a year and so on."

Cynthia Moore added her thoughts. "That's the same as in English," said she. "We talk of Queen Victoria's day, and that would be sixty-four years. We talk of the days of the Romans, and that would be centuries. A new day dawned in America in 1776, and it is still with us, so that would not be twenty-four hours. So I can see this point."

"I don't," said Harry McClelland, bluntly. "The Bible says 'days' and I don't see why we should consider them anything else but days of twenty-four hours."

"There is one good reason," said Fitzgerald, the geology student. "Take a look at the Grand Canyon. The Colorado River has cut deep and exposed stratum after stratum of sandstone and limestone going back millions of years, and you tell me that all this took place in six days."

"God could have done it in six days," replied Harry, stubbornly.

"God could have done it," said Phil Weber, "in six seconds. The question is not what God could have done, but what God actually did. And the record of the rocks shows us that it took a long time."

"Why is it," asked Harry, rather bitterly, "that for centuries Christians have believed that Creation was accomplished in six literal days, and now some of them are willing to take them as ages just to accommodate sceptics?"

"Hold on, old boy," said Micnael. "Fifteen or more centuries ago, Augustine declared that 'the length of these days is not to be determined by the length of our week-days; there is a series in both cases, and that is all.' I do not take all my theology from Saint Augustine, but I accept this as showing that there was this opinion fifteen hundred years ago."

"This is the view," added Houston MacNeill, "least opposed by secular scientists and more and more supported by evangelistic scientists."

"Why then does it say," asked Harry, quickly, " 'the evening and the morning were the first day,' 'the evening and the morning were the second day,' 'the evening and the morning were the third day,' and so on?"

"That's a Hebrew expression," said Michael, "meaning the beginning and the end of a period. The Hebrews started their days in the evening. And even that expression is used symbolically for a longer period in the prophecy of Daniel."

Chapter 13

HOW DID GOD CREATE?

"**M**y professor says," said Harry, "that where the Bible uses an ordinal number before the word 'yom,' it must mean a literal twenty-four hours."

"Look, old boy," replied Michael. "We have already conceded that the overwhelming use of the word 'yom' in Hebrew as in English signifies either a twelve-hour or twenty-four hour day. And the figurative use for a longer period is the exceptional one. Hence the peculiar use in the story of Creation is most exceptional."

"You're trying to tell me," retorted Harry, "that each of the six days represents a geological age! Very well. Suppose there was a day of a million years. Does that mean that five hundred thousand years were in darkness and five hundred thousand in light, the evening and the morning?"

"Some hold the view that 'days' represented geological ages," said Michael. "And a brilliant Royal

Air Force officer, an ardent evangelical, suggested that the days of Genesis were dictation periods—the time that Moses took dictating the revelation on clay tablets, or some such idea. I mention this to show evangelical latitude.

"I am more inclined," he went on, "to treat the days of Genesis as days of God's decree. I mean, there must have been a day when God said 'Let there be light.' There must have been a day when God said 'Let there be an atmosphere' and there must have been a day when God said 'Let the land masses separate from the oceans.' How much time elapsed between these days of decree no one can say."

"Scientists can estimate," added Phil Weber. He turned to McClelland. "Don't you see, Harry, that the main reason why an evangelical scientist refuses to accept a one-hundred-and-forty-four-hours or six literal days interpretation is that he would be accepting an interpretation of a text of Scripture—an interpretation challenged by Saint Augustine, I have learned—which is flatly contradicted by an established fact of science, namely, that our earth is of great antiquity and that it was a long time in the making."

"But what about the Sabbath?" asked Harry. "What about other scriptural references to the six days? What about them?"

"Augustine said," repeated Stratton-Smith, "that there is a series in both cases and that is all. Just as God brought the heaven and earth into being through six days of decree and then rested, so we are to rest one day in seven."

"That does not satisfy me," said Harry.

"But it satisfies me," said Petersen.

Harry McClelland was finding himself in the center of controversy. He held to his views with a dogged determination born of indoctrination.

"Harry!" challenged Charles Fitzgerald. "If you find the bones of a dinosaur in Arizona, how do you account for it in six-day creation?"

"One explanation," replied Harry, "is this. If we believe that when God created Adam, he made him a young man of twenty-five or so, with a navel, although he did not need a navel . . ."

The men smiled and the girls giggled.

"I'm not joking," said Harry, fiercely. "Could we not believe that when God made this planet, he hid in the rocks the bones of dinosaurs to give them the appearance of age?"

"You're kidding," said Weber.

"He isn't!" said Michael. "One naturalist-expositor taught that God had hidden the fossils in the rocks to test men's faith."

"After all," Harry went on, "when God made the first tree, he must have made it with rings. Okay. Let's say that he made it with a hundred rings, then it looked a hundred years old though it was less than a day old."

"But who says," asked Jack Petersen, "that God created a tree? Allow me to quote the story of Creation in Genesis: 'God said, Let the earth produce vegetation, various kinds of seed-bearing herbs and fruit-bearing trees with their respective seeds in the fruit upon the earth; and so it was.' I quoted the Berkeley Version for you."

"I quoted Augustine earlier," said Michael. "Let me quote him again. 'It often happens that a non-Christian derives from clearest arguments or the evidence of his senses, specific scientific knowledge regarding geography, astronomy, zoology, botany, etc.

" 'It is both improper and mischievous for any Christian man to speak on such matters as if so authorized by Scripture and yet talk so foolishly that the unbeliever, observing the extravagance of his mistakes, is scarcely able to keep from laughing. And the real trouble is not so much that the man is laughed at for his blunders, but that writers of Scripture are believed to have taught such things and are so condemned and rejected as ignorant by people outside the Church, to the great loss of those whose salvation we so desire.

" 'They find one belonging to the Christian body so far wrong on a subject they themselves know so well; and, on top of it, find him enforcing his groundless opinions by the authority of our Holy Bible. So they come to regard the Scriptures as unsound on subjects they have learned by observation or unquestioned evidence. Are they likely therefore to put their trust in these Scriptures about the resurrection of the dead, the hope of eternal life, and the kingdom of heaven?' "

"There's the real problem," said Petersen. "It's not just a matter of interpretation against interpretation. It is driving students away. It is giving the unbeliever a chance to scoff. And it is jeopardizing the faith of young people."

"This discussion," commented the Chaplain, "seems to have stirred up more feeling than usual. I have been thinking it over. It might be profitable for all of us to discuss the theories of Creation that a Christian student is likely to encounter in his university or college classes."

There was immediate agreement.

"Do you find," asked the Chaplain, "that the students are interested in this subject?"

"Yes and no," answered Weber. "Many of them consider the question closed, that the Bible has been discredited except as pious writing. I find that students who are interested are those who are interested in Christianity personally, either professional atheists anxious to attack or evangelistic believers anxious to defend or uncommitted Christians anxious to find a harmony of science and Scripture."

"Will it be possible to arrive at some kind of final harmony of science and Scripture?"

The Chaplain answered Liu's question. "A harmony of science and Scripture deemed most acceptable today might be completely outdated within thirty years, due chiefly to the endless revisions of scientific conclusions. When scientists finally, if ever, settle their debates, it may be possible to harmonize their conclusions with the revealed truth of Scripture, providing expositors likewise agree among themselves!"

Harry McClelland coughed nervously.

The Chaplain went on. "You ask me why? First of all, who can tell what scientists may hold at the turn of the next century? My harmony may satisfy me today, but it would have been unintelligible to Martin Luther or John Wesley, both of whom had very fine minds but who were strongly influenced by then current scientific notions. After all, those churchmen who condemned Galileo received all their astronomical notions, not from the Bible but from Ptolemy. They had dyed-in-the-wool conservative ideas about a lot of things besides astronomy. Yes, Harry?"

"Some of the boys," he said, "gave me a bad

time this session. No ill-feeling, of course. But I would like to bring two classmates with me to lend me some moral support. Both have quite a few ideas of their own. One is Jerry Jansen, an 'A' student in almost everything. The other is a good fellow too—Ted Bond."

"They'll be very welcome."

Chapter 14

IS EVERYBODY WRONG?

"**C**haplain," began Michael Stratton-Smith, "there are so many theories of Creation that I suggest that we limit discussion to the six most likely to be encountered. I have made notes:

"First, atheistic spontaneous evolution; and second, pantheistic eternal evolution of the universe. I contend that both these theories are impossible for a Christian to hold, on two counts. Third, deistic mediate evolution; fourth, theistic immediate creation. I contend that each of these views has a strength and weakness. Fifth, theistic immediate re-creation; sixth, theistic progressive creation, both popular harmonies."

Cynthia Moore looked up helplessly at Helen Johnson. The technical terms bothered her, but she was mollified when the Chaplain suggested that Michael should write the terms on a board and explain them.

"All right," said Nils Andersson. "I'll ask. What major theory held by some philosophers is utterly impossible for a Christian to accept on both scriptural and scientific grounds?"

"We have really discussed this before," said Michael, evenly. "It arose in our discussion of the repugnance of chance."

"I wasn't here," said Fritz Wagner.

"The theory of atheistic spontaneous evolution—that matter and life evolved by chance without God," explained Weber, "is clearly contradicted by the scriptural claim that God initiated and superintended the creation and development of the world of matter and life; and blind chance, as said before, is repugnant to common sense."

"I missed that," said Fritz Wagner. "The 'repugnant to common sense' bit."

"We can't go over the whole argument again," said Stratton-Smith. "Some one will give you his notes. But may I tell a wizard story? I don't necessarily vouch for it.

"There was a professor at Oxford University who held the view that a team of chimpanzees, typing on a set of typewriters, sooner or later would strike off all the great classics, including Shakespeare. Extraordinary, what?

"A professor of such erudition, of course, was much too busy to superintend the typewriting of chimpanzees. So he assigned the work to his students, who made a daily report to him in term and even during vacation. After seventeen years, a Merton man called him up to make his report by telephone. 'Are you there?' he began. 'Sir, I wish to report that another of the monkeys has died of old age.' "

There was loud laughter, but Michael went on. "The student continued his report: 'Sir. Another of the monkeys refuses to type any more.'"

The laughter was renewed.

"'But the other ten are typing away, sir . . . No, sir. I cannot understand a word of what they are typing. In fact, the letters they are typing do not make words, sir . . .'"

Everyone was listening keenly.

"'Except number seven, sir,' the student went on. 'Number Seven's typing is extraordinary. Shall I read it to you, sir? Very well. "To be or not to be, that . is . . the . . . unzinquatsch".'"

After the laughter subsided, Adams said, "Okay. That's one count. The repugnance of chance. What's the other?"

"That's simple," replied Weber. "Atheistic spontaneous evolution is utterly impossible for a Christian, because he cannot be an atheist."

"What other popular theory taught by some philosophers is utterly impossible for a Christian to accept on both counts?" asked Andersson.

"The theory of pantheistic eternal evolution," answered Stratton-Smith. "In other words, making the universe equivalent to God and without beginning. That is contradicted by the Scriptures as well as by the sound deductions of science already cited."

"Excuse me," said Fitzgerald. "What sound deductions of science? I wasn't here during that discussion."

"I'll give you my notes," offered Weber, "on the first and second laws of thermodynamics. Scientists agree that the sun, for example, had a beginning and will come to an end. It is assumed that this applies to the universe, and the critics of the view have produced no evidence against it."

"What is 'pantheistic'?" asked Zefani, the Zulu.

"That's the idea that all is God and God is all," answered Michael. "Some oriental philosophers teach that God is good and God is evil, God is day and God is night, God is kind and God is cruel, God is pure and God is impure, that God is the sum total of the universe, and that everything that happens is God. But the Scripture teaches that 'God is light and in him is no darkness at all,' and this is the message we have received from Christ. You cannot be a Christian and a pantheist, though of course there is truth in the idea that God pervades everything. The Christian believes that God is greater than his works."

"So both of those theories," commented Helen Johnson, "are impossible for a Christian on two counts. What are these next two theories?"

"The next two have one thing in common," explained Michael. "That is, that one may accept either and be a Christian. Or, put it in this way. Known evangelical Christians have accepted one or other and maintained a Christian faith. But either theory has a weakness, one scientific and the other scriptural."

"All right then," said Bonelli. "The other side. What popular theory has been held by many practicing Christians but is in conflict with the clear text of Scripture?"

"What popular theory has been held by many practicing Christians but is in conflict with the established facts of science?" asked Adams.

"The theory of theistic immediate creation," replied Weber, "a creation popularly held to have occurred in 4004 B.C. by fiat in a space of one-hundred-and-forty-four hours. To my mind, it ignores the Genesis verbs of indirect action and conflicts with the well-established conclusions of science that the earth is thousands of times older and its formation took millions of times longer."

"You know," interrupted Jack Petersen. "My grandmother held this view, and she was a saint."

"But did anyone seriously teach this?" asked Nils Andersson.

"Not only did Archbishop Ussher teach that the world was created in 4004 B.C.," said Michael, "but Lightfoot of Cambridge taught that Adam was created at nine o'clock on the morning of the twenty-third of October, 4004 B.C. Mesopotamia standard time. As a careful scholar, Lightfoot was unable to commit himself further than that."

"But where did Archbishop Ussher get his figures?" asked Helen Johnson.

"I suppose," replied Petersen, "that he added together all the ages of the patriarchs and so arrived at his estimate. And what is wrong with that? Scholars are not satisfied that the list of the earliest patriarchs is comprised of fathers-and-sons."

"Why not?"

"Well, for one thing, the Hebrew expression 'son of' or the verb 'begat' do not necessarily imply a father-and-son relationship. Even the genealogy of Jesus Christ in the first Gospel, Matthew, describes him as 'son of David, son of Abraham.' Taking that literally would mean that he was a grandson of Abraham."

"What is the great objection against such a theory?" asked Adams.

"It is this," responded Philip Weber. "Let us say

that we have two possible interpretations. One is in harmony with established conclusions of science and the other is contradicted by them. One says 'In the beginning' means an indefinite time ago, and the other that it means six thousand years ago, and the latter view was taught by one who knew nothing of geology. What must we do? I have chosen the indefinite view. You can be a good husband and father and citizen and neighbor and believe that Adam was born on October 23 in 4004 B.C., but you will be a poor scientist."

Many in the class had expected an interruption from Harry McClelland in this argument, but no comment came. Harry sat at ease, with a good-natured smile on his face.

"The theory of deistic mediate evolution, yet to be considered," said Stratton-Smith, "is that God gave creation its initial impulse but left it to develop solely through the inherent forces of nature. This is in conflict with the plain statements of Genesis that record God's progressive participation in creation."

"That's the main objection," said Weber. "It can also be said that pure science does not at all demand that God had no part in the expansion of the universe and the development of life on earth. Most scientists will agree that some mysterious force caused such developments."

"What evangelical Christians, if any, held this view?" asked Harry McClelland, breaking his silence at last.

"For example," said the Texan, MacNeill, "there was James Orr of Edinburgh. He was a Presbyterian. And there was Augustus Strong of Rochester.

He was a Baptist. Both of them were undoubted evangelicals. There are others."

"I noticed, Michael," commented Petersen, "that you referred to 'deistic' rather than to 'theistic mediate evolution.' Why?"

"Well," replied the Englishman, "when my over-cautious friends attack the idea of theistic mediate evolution, they generally mean deistic mediate evolution. Perhaps it should be said that Orr and Strong and others like them held a theistic rather than a deistic view. In fact, there is a certain amount of theistic evolution in the next two harmonies."

Chapter 15

WHAT SHALL I BELIEVE?

"What suggested harmony between scientific theory and biblical interpretation is popular in some circles today?" asked Rafferty Jones.

It was Michael Stratton-Smith who replied. "The theory of theistic immediate re-creation has been popularized by the Scofield Bible. It is popularly known as the 'Gap Theory' and teaches two creations, one in Genesis 1:1 and another in Genesis 1:2 the latter taking one-hundred-and-forty-four hours or six literal days.

"Of course," continued Michael, "it is hard to represent properly the views of those who hold the 'Gap Theory.' Some, apparently, hold that the words 'In the beginning' permit not only an indeterminate number of years to predate Creation, but that most of the geological record of evolutionary process may be fitted therein."

Jerry Jansen cleared his throat. "The advantage,"

he began, "of the re-creation theory is that it gives us all the time that we need for the geological record and at the same time allows us to hold to the word of Scripture."

"Do you accept the geological record then?" asked Charles Fitzgerald.

"Up to the catastrophe implied in verse two," replied Jansen.

"But then you must place the radiation of light, the separation of the continents from the oceans, the production of a self-propagating vegetation, the emergence of life in the oceans, appearance of birds in the air, and development of mammals on the land all in a week following the billions of years of what? I don't understand."

"Did the dinosaurs," asked Weber, "inhabit the earth before or after this catastrophe?"

"Perhaps the dinosaurs were drowned in the Flood," suggested Harry McClelland.

"I'm willing to accept a flood," said Weber. "There's enough clay in Mesopotamia to support that. But there is no geographical evidence for believing that dinosaurs were drowned in it. You can't have it both ways."

"Suppose I say that I believe that dinosaurs roamed the earth between verses one and two in Genesis chapter one," replied Jerry, carefully. "That would allow for the re-creation of all the life destroyed in the catastrophe."

"It is surely strange," said Michael, "that the first verse of Genesis does not mention this earlier world of physical beings. On what do you base the theory, from a biblical point of view?"

"The Hebrew word 'was' may be translated 'became' in the second verse, making it 'and the earth became without form and void.' "

"With all due respect," said Michael, politely, "I cannot accept the interpretation. I don't know of a reputable Hebrew scholar amongst Jews or Protestants or Roman Catholics admitting it."

"There are supporting scriptures," replied Jerry. "There is Jeremiah chapter four, verse twenty-three. There is Isaiah forty-five, verse eighteen."

There was a turning of pages, and Cynthia Moore offered to read the Jeremiah quotation.

"Read the whole paragraph," said Michael. "Read from verse nineteen to verse thirty-one."

Cynthia read the lament in a clear treble. It described the destruction of Judah by invaders, with the spoiling of the land, the desolated cities, the orchards a wilderness, even the birds fled.

"What has this to do with Genesis?" she asked. "What is the connection?"

"You see that single phrase," said Michael, "that the earth was 'without form and void'? It is the same phrase for chaos in Hebrew as that used to describe the condition of the earth when it was first created."

"Others teach that when in the indeterminate beginning, God created the earth," said Weber, "he made it a perfect Garden of Eden. This is another interpretation of the 'Gap Theory.' "

"Read Isaiah chapter forty-five, eighteen!" requested Ted Bond.

Cynthia speedily obliged.

"You see," said Bond. "God did not create the earth a chaos. He formed it to be inhabited. He must have made it perfect. Then it became a chaos a long time afterwards."

"Excuse me," interrupted Weber. "I do not think that God finished creating until the end of the sixth day. By that time, it was a cosmos and not a chaos. But that it was a chaos at the very beginning is stated in the opening verses of the Genesis account, and this is fully confirmed by the latest scientific opinion."

"Both schools of thought holding the Gap Theory," said Jansen, "say that there was a rebellion in the heavenly host of angels, led by Satan, and that this brought the earth to ruin, without form and void."

"That may be the case regarding the angels, but it is questionable regarding the earth," replied Weber.

"The reason that I object to the Gap Theory," said Michael, "is that it scraps the majesty of the order of God's creation held by Christians for so long, and substitutes a re-creation which it restricts to one-hundred-and-forty-four hours—and that presents us with a story of creation flatly contradicted by those who have studied the rocks and the fossils."

"Besides which," added Petersen, "the idea of a catastrophic gap has flimsy scriptural support, being read into Genesis and taken out of its context in Jeremiah 4:23 and misinterpreted in Isaiah 45:18, while the geological records lend no scientific support at all."

"I still disagree," said Jerry, firmly.

"Very well," said the Chaplain. "Let us take note of the sixth school of thought."

"What other harmony between Scripture and science is popular among other evangelicals?" asked Rafferty Jones.

"The theory of theistic progressive creation attributes to God," said Phil Weber, "successive acts of creation as well as intermediate, indirect processes of development."

"What are its advantages?" asked Adams.

"This harmony," said Michael, "is least in conflict with the facts of science and the text of Scripture. It enables a Christian student to become a good scientist following truth wherever it may lead, yet it treats the Creation story as revealed truth."

"And its disadvantages?"

"It leaves many questions unanswered."

"Chaplain," said Zefani Mhlongwa. "In what shall I believe?"

"You will have to decide for yourself," said the Chaplain. "You cannot hold the atheistic or pantheistic views and be a Christian. You could hold either deistic evolution or fiat creation and be an otherwise devoted Christian, but you will be either a poor scientist or poor Bible student. You can choose between the two harmonies, but you will have to meet the difficulties inherent in each. You will have to say simply that you do not know when you are asked some questions."

Chapter 16

CAN ANYONE KNOW GOD?

The Chaplain had noticed that the Chinese engineer had followed the discussion of the theories of Creation with great interest. He had shown a tolerant patience with the debaters, even when they displayed a far from scientific attitude. It was not surprising that the next session opened with another statement from P. T. Liu.

"Chaplain," he said, "I would like to say that my convictions are deepening and my views are clarifying. I am not ready to accept the Christian faith. I don't know enough about it. But I think that I can declare myself a theist, a believer in a Supreme Being."

"Excellent," said the Chaplain. "I think that you will find that our discussions will take you into a totally different realm, the knowledge of God. Let me say again that science can tell us nothing about

99

God. We must look for information elsewhere, obviously."

"Okay," said David Adams. "I'll go along. What kind of a revelation of truth may we expect from God?"

"Our knowledge of God in nature," said the Chaplain, "would lead us to expect a revelation of truth which would not contradict what we have learned from nature."

The Chaplain paused to let the point sink in. David Adams was quick to appreciate it.

"That's a good idea," he said. "Now you're talking. I'm beginning to get sorted out."

"You mean," said P. T. Liu, "there should be a parallel between scientific and scriptural presentation of truth?"

"Just as nature unfolds its lessons in graded steps, so there ought to be a continuous historical development of the greater spiritual truths," added the Chaplain.

"What puzzles me is this," said Andersson. "How would we expect scriptural revelation to be authenticated as coming from God and not from man? I mean, what's to prevent someone trading his own philosophy as divine revelation? There are non-Christian systems which contradict in effect the Christian revelation, yet they claim to be revelations from God."

"Divine revelation," stated Stratton-Smith, "bears the marks of its divine authorship. It is recognizable as a message of God's truth rather than human thought, for it honestly records the sins and failures of its heroes. Its bearers were attested by God with signs such as miracles or prophecy. All that I have said applies to the Holy Scriptures."

"I have so much to learn," commented P. T. Liu. "I know so little of the Bible. I am happy to say that I want to learn now."

"Okay," said Bonelli. "It raises a question. How would the record of God's revelation to men be best preserved for generations to come?"

Helen Johnson raised her hand. "I think that it is obvious," she began, "that the best method of preserving and passing on the revelation of God would be by means of written records given by those persons receiving it."

". . . copied by others with meticulous care," added Houston MacNeill.

"This was the method used to preserve the books of the Bible," Helen concluded.

"I too have a question," said Rafferty Jones. "Does history demonstrate the value of the divine revelation in Scripture? I am not talking about fulfilled prophecies. I mean moral benefit."

"Pagan nations," said the Chaplain, "without divine revelation in ancient times deteriorated, through corruption as in the fall of pagan Rome. Evangelized nations gladly receiving the truth were helped thereby—as in the rise of modern Britain, when its people 'became a people of the Book.' There are many examples of this."

"In what way," asked P. T. Liu, "may Holy Scripture as a revelation be said to differ from other literature?"

"A serious student can see," said Michael, "that the Bible, though written by many authors over many centuries, is not only a great work in the science of humanity but is the work of one Mind with a unity of spirit, subject and object through-out. This is most amazing."

"Are you trying to tell me," asked Adams, "that only the Bible has truth? What about the eightfold way of Buddhism?"

"The eightfold way in Buddhism," said the Chaplain, "is excellent as moral philosophy."

"I'm glad you're not narrow-minded," said Bonelli. "One way is as good as another."

"What is the supreme revelation of God?" asked the Chaplain. He answered his question. "Truths taught in other religions have often been obscured or corrupted, and truths revealed by the prophets before Christ were often incomplete or imperfect. But, it is obvious, the truth revealed in Jesus Christ has never been surpassed. That is the supreme revelation of God."

"Earlier Michael mentioned miracles. What is a miracle?" asked Fritz Wagner.

"A miracle," answered Michael, "is an extraordinary event in nature not necessarily apart from the use of natural forces produced by the direct operation of God's power in support of the message of his messenger, to secure its acceptance and certification to others."

"That's much too fast for me," protested Liu. "I don't understand miracles. I am an engineer. I know what I mean by an extraordinary event. Was the evacuation of Dunkirk by the British a miracle? Extraordinary, yes, but miracle?"

"With all due respect to British patriotism," said the Chaplain, "let's call it an extraordinary event, and a very providential one from the point of view of the whole anti-Hitler Alliance."

"Notice again what I said," continued Michael. "A miracle is produced by the direct operation of God's power, therefore he must have a stake in the outcome in a special sense. And it is in support of the message of his prophet or apostle to secure its acceptance by others. Therefore the best examples I can find are from the Old and New Testaments— say, the miracles of the prophet Elijah at Mount Carmel or of the apostle Peter at the Temple Gate."

"I just don't understand miracles," grumbled Bonelli. "This really stretches my credulity."

"Let me tell you all a story," said Michael. "There was a Methodist minister in England who was working so hard that his wife told him that he was due for a nervous break-down. The good parson promised her that as soon as Conference was over, they would take a holiday in Scotland. The minister missed the last train home, but caught another train to a junction only five miles away. It was a beautiful moonlit night as he started walking home. He was dead tired. He ached in every limb. But he felt relieved the strain was all over, and a holiday lay ahead. He was thinking about Scotland when suddenly he heard a lion roar.

"Now this chap knew enough about England to know that lions do not roar in that blessed plot. He had heard lions roar in Kenya. So he decided that he imagined things. Then he heard the lion roar again. He stopped dead.

"Now the parson felt a rising tide of alarm. He was imagining things. His wife was right; he was near a nervous break-down. He stood listening, straining his ears for sounds and his eyes for any movement in the moonlight. He walked forward

103

again, his heart thumping. Suddenly, he heard a blood-curdling roar, and he thought he saw a full-maned, tawny lion break out of the bushes a hundred yards ahead, and stand there with lashing tail.

"The Methodist parson retreated. He walked backwards step by step. When he backed into a tree at a turn in the road, he panicked, took to his heels and ran full tilt back to the railway station, where he waited for the early milk-train back to London.

"He checked in at a hotel, sent a telegram to his wife to say that he was delayed a day, took a dose of sleeping pills and slept twenty-four hours. He wakened fully expecting to realize that it had been some kind of nightmare. But it still seemed real. He was planning to make an appointment with a psychiatrist when there was a rustling at the door. Someone pushed a morning paper under the door. He picked it up and read on the front page that all the animals that had escaped from the derailment of the circus train had now been recaptured.

"Now he understood that his eyes and ears had not deceived him when he disbelieved them. But why did he disbelieve them? He had brought to the evidence a predisposition to disbelieve that lions roared in the English countryside. So in one way, the philosophy we bring to the facts is often more influential in deciding our judgment than evidence of eyewitnesses or the senses."

"In my case," added Philip Weber, "I can believe a miracle if it accompanies a message from God. If anyone here claimed to raise the dead, I would have my doubts. That Christ raised the dead I am satisfied, for there were many eyewitnesses and I know that Christ was God's son."

104

"You said, Michael, there was another sign. What is prophecy?" asked Fitzgerald.

Michael Stratton-Smith gave a definition. "Prophecy is the foretelling of future events—often with reference to events separated in time—by the immediate agency of God's foreknowledge in keeping with the message of his messenger, to influence the course of action of the hearers."

"But has there been any actual foretelling of events?" asked Charles, curiously. "I mean, any authenticated instance of prophecy?"

"Say," said Lt. Petersen. "Did you ever read Lord Tennyson—'Saw the nations airy navies grappling in the central blue'—written in Queen Victoria's day. Boy, I thought of that in combat, up in the wild blue yonder."

"That," said Michael, "is the foretelling of events by human foresight. Prophecy is the foretelling of events by God's foreknowledge and in connection with a message to prepare for action of some sort. That is Bible prophecy."

"Can you give us any example of a prophecy fulfilled, a Bible prophecy, a clear one?" asked Fitzgerald, sincerely.

"Oh, dear yes," responded Michael. "There are at least fifty passages of the Old Testament Scriptures fulfilled regarding Christ in the New. In Ezekiel chapter twenty-six, the Lord God tells the city of Tyre that he will bring many nations against it, in waves, that they would destroy the walls of Tyre and scrape her soil from her and make her a bare rock, a place for the spreading of nets. This was fulfilled in the destruction of the famous maritime city by Nebuchadnezzar and again by Alexander the Great, so that today it is desolate rocks, where fishermen spread nets."

"We must never forget," said the Chaplain, "that the Scriptures are a revelation of God. In Christ the revelation is unsurpassed."

Chapter 17

WHO SAYS IT'S THE BIBLE?

"I am beginning to see," said Lt. Jack Petersen, "where this discussion is leading. You have shown that faith in God is a universal human insight, agreeable to reason; now we are moving to show that it is verified by revelation and confirmed by experience."

"Here is my first question," said P. T. Liu. "How do we learn the truths revealed in Christ?"

"That deserves a simple answer," said Ted. "The life and works and teachings of Christ are revealed to us through the uncontested records of eyewitnesses, in the Gospels and Epistles written by these apostles or those who wrote on their behalf."

"Excuse me," P. T. Liu interrupted. "I have read many obvious legends about the birth of the Buddha. Are there not legends about Jesus also? How do we know that these records contained in the

New Testament are fact and not legend, as so often is the case in other religions?"

"I have a suggestion on that," said Bonelli. "Take the legend of George Washington and the cutting down of the cherry tree. That has been taught as gospel truth for generations. How many children have heard that George Washington said: 'Sir, I cannot tell a lie'! Well, my history professor gave me a paper to write on that story. I was dumfounded. Did you know that nobody had ever heard of that story during the eighteenth century? You might say that perhaps it had been circulating by word of mouth, but you must weigh against that idea the discovery that it was first published by a writer of pious fiction for children."

"That's a good point," commented Michael. "And that's how many legends grew up in other religions and a few in extra-evangelical church tradition. The New Testament writings however were in wide and uncontested circulation among Christians before the decease of all these eyewitnesses or apostles. The fact that these letters and narratives were already in circulation at the end of the first century, within a lifetime of the crucifixion of Christ, takes them out of the category of legends, don't you think?"

"Suppose a Communist dictator," said Jerry, "were to order the destruction of every Greek manuscript of the New Testament and every last translation, but did not know enough to destroy the writings of the earliest fathers who followed the apostles, we could reconstruct the whole of the New Testament from the writings of these early fathers, except for eight verses."

"In other words," commented Stratton-Smith, "a

cross-reference of quotations made by the Christian writers in immediate post-apostolic years covers all but a few verses of the New Testament. The verses are in John's Gospel."

"That's very interesting," commented Cynthia, "but how can the Gospels and Epistles be dated?"

"The evidence for the dates is self-contained in many instances," explained the Chaplain. "For example, Christ's predictions of the destruction of Jerusalem were not reported as fulfilled in the Synoptic Gospels, Matthew, Mark and Luke, so they must have been written before A.D. 70."

"The various quotations by later writers also suggest dates," added Houston MacNeill.

"Hold on a minute," said David Adams. "I was on board ship with a minister of a church—not an evangelical one or a Catholic one—and he told me that nobody could vouch for the Gospel of John. Is it not said that the Gospel of John was penned by an unknown writer hundreds of years later?"

"This theory, recently popular," said Weber, "is thoroughly discredited by the latest modern scholarship which, using modern findings and research, now assigns a date in the eighties of the first century to the Gospel of John confirming historic tradition. There has never been a finer vindication of the canon of Scripture."

The Swedish engineer spoke up. "How was the New Testament compiled and its accepted form completed?"

"May I answer this?" asked Ted Bond. "The Gospels and Epistles were circulated singly in the first century, and they were circulated in the second century collectively. But three centuries after Christ, church authorities found it necessary to distinguish between the clearly apostolic documents on one hand and the both genuine and spurious post-apostolic writings on the other. So they checked these against quotations made by the friends and companions and successors of the apostles, comparing also their doctrinal contents with the accepted writings."

"It reminds me," said the Chaplain, "that I was once addressing a crowd of students at the California Institute of Technology. That school reputedly has the highest I.Q. average in the country. A bright lad asked me, 'Is it not a fact that the New Testament that we have today was put into its present form in the fourth century?'

" 'The canon was completed then,' I replied.

" 'Is it not a fact that there was a Gospel of Peter and a Gospel of Thomas?'

" 'Yes, and the Shepherd of Hermas and the teaching of the Twelve Apostles.'

" 'Why weren't they included in the canon?'

" 'Well, it was found that no one in the early days had ever heard of these psuedo-Gospels. The Gospel of Thomas appeared to be a pious fraud. It told stories of the childhood of Jesus, making him perform silly actions. So these were dropped as pious frauds. The other two that I mentioned, however, were genuine but were not written by the apostles or on apostolic authority. They are still read for their historical and their doctrinal value as post-apostolic information. But they were not included in the canon.'

" 'Is it not a fact that the bishops and fathers of the church decided what would go into the New Testament? Does not that mean that the authority rests in the church and not in the Scriptures?'

" 'No, sir,' I replied. 'But tell me the story as you heard it.'

"The student grinned and said, 'As I heard it, there were a lot of scriptures floating around, some genuine, some otherwise. So the bishops and fathers of the church put the genuine and the disputed books on the floor, and prayed over them, where-upon the genuine ones jumped by themselves onto the table.' I told him that his story was inaccurate."

"What I would like to know is this," said Liu. "Why are there four Gospels and why the minor discrepancies between them?"

"The four Gospels," replied Ted Bond, "seem to be suited to four different constituencies, the Jew-ish, the Roman, the Greek and the churchly. It is not a weakness to have four Gospels. If you were to take me to court and produce four eyewitnesses to say the same thing in support of you, the judge would suspect collusion. In an accident, the police-man, the pedestrian, the driver and the passenger all see things from a slightly different point of view. Putting four testimonies together enables us to see with historical perspective."

"The testimonies of four witnesses," repeated Michael, "from four points of view provide real strength rather than weakness, while the minor discrepancies, not contradictions, between them strengthen their credibility and discount charges of collusion or faked agreement."

"What sort of discrepancies?" asked Adams.

"Well, for example," explained Phil Weber, "in the Gospel of Matthew, chapter eight, is the story of the healing of the centurion's son. In this ac-count, it says that the centurion personally besought the Lord to say the word. In the Gospel of Luke, chapter seven, it says that he sent elders of the Jews and then sent friends. Now which did he do? He may have done both, though the story in Luke seems to invalidate that interpretation. It may be that Dr. Luke gives the more detailed narrative, and that Matthew gives a shortened version, as though what one does through others he does himself responsibly. Who knows? The integrity of the story is not affected. We should avoid pitfalls—one, that of pretending that there are no apparent discrepancies; two, using minor discrepancies to discredit the essential truth of the narrative given with perspective."

Chapter 18

DO I HAVE
ALL THE BIBLE?

"I see that our numbers are growing," said the Chaplain. "This room will soon be too small. Who are our friends today?"

Responded Helen Johnson, "I brought two Latin American friends. May I present a Brazilian student, Julio Vasconceles Filho of Niteroi . . ."

"Hi, Mr. Filho," said Ted Bond.

Senhor Julio smiled a tolerant smile.

"Excuse me," said the Chaplain. "We are delighted to welcome Mr. Vasconceles to our group. The suffix 'Filho,'" he added in an aside to Ted Bond, "means 'son,' somewhat like our 'junior.' So addressing a Brazilian as Mr. Filho is like addressing an American as Mr. Junior."

"My mistake," said Bond, with a laugh.

"However," continued the Chaplain, "no doubt in Brazil our friend is known as Senhor Julio, so he will not mind us calling him Julio."

Senhor Julio bowed in agreement. Helen went on with her introductions. "And this is Hernando Garcia O'Brien of Los Vilos, Republic of Chile."

"O'Brien?" queried Harry McClelland.

"That was my mother's name," explained the Chilean. "My family name is Garcia. There is some Irish blood in Chile. Our liberator was Bernardo O'Higgins. But you call me Hernando."

"Very well," said the Chaplain. "What is our topic for today?"

"I would like to ask," said Rafferty Jones, "does the revelation of God in the Old Testament compare with the revelation of God in the New?"

The Chaplain turned to the Negro runner. "Why do you ask that question?"

"Well," said he, "I hear people talk about the God of the Old Testament or Yawveh as if he were some other sort of God."

"To my mind," responded the Chaplain, "the God who created the heaven and earth is the same God who is revealed in Christ. Perhaps the people before Christ came did not understand him. The Old Testament may be considered as an unfolding revelation whereas the New Testament is an unsurpassed revelation of God. What was concealed in the Old is revealed in the New, and what was incomplete in the Old is fulfilled in the New. Both Testaments present the same God and announce his provision for man's need."

"We examined the New Testament canon," said Helen. "What about the Old? How do we know that the Old Testament books are genuine?"

"Ancient and modern Jewish authorities treat the Old Testament as a sacred book, and it was translated as such into Greek by Alexandrian Jews two centuries before Christ," he replied.

"To this is added the testimony of Christ and of his apostles," added Jerry Jansen. "Nearly all these books are quoted directly in the New Testament. Josephus in the first century cited all but two of the books as 'justly accredited.'"

"You mean," commented David Adams, "that the Old Testament is sacred literature to both Jews and Christians?"

"And to Moslems," added Rafferty Jones. "I heard them refer to the Torah and the Injil and to Christians as 'people of the Book.'"

"How was the Old Testament compiled," Nils Andersson asked, "and why are the books of the Apocrypha omitted from its finished form?"

"The Apocrypha was included in the Roman Catholic Bible," said Cynthia Moore.

"I would like to answer that," said Michael Stratton-Smith. "Just as New Testament books were written by the apostles or their penmen and committed to the Christian Church for protection and recognition, so the Old Testament books were written by the prophets and committed to the people of Israel for protection and recognition. The apocryphal books written after the end of the prophetic period were refused recognition by the rabbis and experts in Jewish law."

"So that is why the books of the Apocrypha are omitted from the Authorized Version," said Charles Fitzgerald. "Why are they retained in the Douai Version?"

"Some doctrines not taught in the Old or New Testaments are found there," said McClelland.

115

"Let me ask this," ventured P. T. Liu. "Why was the Old Testament revelation of God given to the Hebrew people rather than to other nations?"

"I suppose," suggested Lt. Petersen, "each nation has its genius, the Greek for art and philosophy, the Roman for law and organization, and God gave the Hebrews a genius for religion, in which they were unique."

"Do you mean that they were better than any other people?" asked Zefani Mhlongwa.

"No," replied Petersen. "They often failed their God. But he called them, choosing them to receive the revelation of his truth until in time it was relayed to all nations by apostles of the same Hebrew stock."

"It is amazing what the Bible says about the Jews," said Harry McClelland. "It denounces them for their failures, and predicts a scattering among all nations, followed by persecution. And yet they were to remain distinct, and be restored to their own land in due course."

"The Old Testament is a Hebrew book," said Rafferty Jones. "What should be the attitude of a Christian to it? Didn't you call it the unfolding revelation of the Old Testament?"

"Why not then adopt the attitude of Christ?" replied the Chaplain. "A Christian should adopt the examples of Christ and his apostles, who treated the Old Testament writings as authentic and authoritative, quoting them precisely as to concept, though less exactly as to letter."

"What do you mean?" asked Jones.

"The quotations," said Michael, "in various instances differ from both the original Hebrew and

116

its Septuagint Greek translation in wording. We can draw our own conclusions."

"Do you mean, Michael," protested Harry Mc-Clelland, "that these quotations are not truly accurate? Are they not inspired?"

"Of course, they are inspired, old boy," said Michael, cheerfully. "Let's just take things as we find them. The Old Testament says one thing in certain words, and the New Testament writers quote the same thing in other words. Do you want to make an issue out of that?"

Harry looked at Jerry Jansen and Ted Bond, then lapsed into silence again.

"Someone said," P. T. Liu recalled, "that the Bible, though written by many different authors over many centuries, possesses a unique unity. Would you say that the Old and New Testaments, the Jewish and Christian Scriptures, form a true unity in that sense?"

"Yes," replied Philip Weber. "It is a unity, and yet it is a library of books."

"Who is the author," asked the Chinese, "and what is the subject of the whole Bible, this Book of books?"

"The ultimate author is the Spirit of God," replied the Chaplain, "who moved men of God to speak and write his message, and I think you could add, its pre-eminent subject is God revealed to man in Jesus Christ the Saviour."

"Can anyone understand the Bible?" asked Helen Johnson.

"It depends on his attitude," replied Michael.

"What is the necessary attitude in the study of the Scriptures?" asked Cynthia.

117

"I would say," replied Jerry Jansen, "that the intellectually proud or morally disobedient may expect to learn little from the Scriptures, for sin blinds the eyes and warps the will. I am sure that there are many who are thus hindered, but whoever is willing to do his will is assured of learning what to believe and how to behave."

"Why is it," asked Cynthia Moore, "that so many people find the Bible a difficult book to read and understand?"

"Let me tell you a story," said the Chaplain. "There was a young evangelist who visited the beautiful city of Durban in South Africa. A lady from Port Shepstone was visiting the city to see a doctor about her back. She attended the meetings and felt moved to write her daughter that she would stay a while longer in Durban to enjoy the campaign. Her daughter was a long-distance-telephonist, and her mother's absence added to her responsibilities. When the mother returned, she was full of the blessing of the campaign, but her daughter was not very interested. Her mother brought several of the evangelist's books for her daughter to read, but the girl was not interested.

"Later that year," continued the Chaplain, "the young lady went to visit her married sister in Johannesburg. There they attended the series of meetings held by the same young evangelist for the Johannesburg Council of Churches.

"To make a long story short," he went on, "the evangelist fell in love with the young lady and later proposed marriage to her. As soon as the young lady arrived back at home, she asked her mother, 'Where are those books?'"

"And what happened?" asked Cynthia Moore.

"They lived happily ever afterwards," said the Chaplain, with a twinkle in his eye. "To get to know the author makes a lot of difference."

Chapter 19

IS THE BIBLE
THE WORD OF GOD?

"Michael and Harry were talking about the Scriptures being inspired," began P. T. Liu. "I have a question. What do we mean by 'divine inspiration'?"

"Actually," replied Jerry Jansen, "the word 'inspired' is not used in the Greek New Testament. The Greek uses the word 'God-breathed' to describe the influence of God upon the writings of the prophets. By divine inspiration, we mean the influence of the Spirit of God on the minds of writers to accomplish his purpose in recording truths necessary for our salvation."

"Say that again!" said David Adams.

"Say what?" asked Jerry. "The influence of the Spirit of God on the minds of writers to accomplish his purpose in recording the truths necessary for our salvation—and that is divine inspiration."

"That's what I thought you said," retorted Adams,

121

provoking a laugh. "How do you guys get these definitions so pat?"

"We learn them," said Jansen. "You ought to learn them too, once you accept them."

"We had a long discussion already about the Bible not being a textbook of science," said Pat Bonelli. "What is the scope and object of this divine inspiration?"

"In the Second Epistle to Timothy, chapter three, verse sixteen," replied Michael, "Paul the apostle states that all Scripture is inspired by God, and is useful for teaching, for reproof, for correction, for training in doing what is right. That's the Williams' Translation."

"It is therefore," added Weber, "a textbook of religion rather than a model history book or a scientific treatise."

"Okay," said Rafferty Jones. "Do we believe that every word of the Scripture was dictated by God?"

"I have heard people talk like that," said Ted Bond. " 'Every word from cover to cover.' Just like an executive dictating to his stenographer."

"You can soon take care of that idea," said Lt. Petersen. "In the First Epistle to the Corinthians, the apostle Paul says 'It makes me thankful that I didn't actually baptize any of you, except Crispus and Gaius, or perhaps someone would be saying I did it in my own name. Oh, yes, I did baptize Stephanas' family, but I cannot remember anyone else's. Now," he continued, "the apostle begins with a statement, adds a first afterthought, goes on with his application, adds a second afterthought, and then says plainly that he does remember how he baptized but not how many. If his words were being dictated by God, he would have been told exactly how many people he had baptized. It seems obvious. When the Holy Spirit inspired the apostle Paul to write that letter for our edification, he allowed him the latitude of his memory."

"But he was inspired," added McClelland.

"Of course, he was inspired," replied the pilot. "But he was not dictated to in a corner."

"I was once talking to a minister," said Helen Johnson, "and he told me: 'Of course, the Bible is inspired. It truly inspires me, so I know it is inspired.'"

"That will never do," protested Phil Weber. "Where would we draw the line? We could say that Shakespeare was inspired, that Kipling was inspired, that Hemingway was inspired. Oh yes, they were inspired in a literary sense but not in our definition of divine inspiration."

P. T. Liu returned to his notes. Said he, "Harry and Michael, I noticed, were arguing about a degree or measure of inspiration. I want to ask this question. Are there varieties of such divine inspiration in the Scriptures?"

"Oh boy," interjected Houston MacNeill. "I think we are going to get technical."

"What do you mean?" asked Bonelli.

"Look at Michael and his notes!"

"Yes, indeed," said the Englishman. "I do have notes and it is a bit technical. But we must face it, don't you think?"

"Must face what?" asked Harry McClelland.

"That there are different kinds of inspiration in the Scripture!"

"But it is all inspired!" protested Harry.

"Oh yes, old boy," replied Michael, evenly. "It is all inspired."

The Chaplain, knowing that Harry viewed the Englishman's theology with a vague suspicion, intervened with a word.

"Suppose," he suggested, "that Michael give us the different varieties of inspiration in the Scriptures, and then we can analyze them and sum it all up?"

"Better still, sir," replied Michael, "to let members of the class suggest different kinds of inspiration and I'll try and classify them. There are three kinds of inspiration, to my way of thinking. Divine inspiration is recorded through an outer verbal revelation, a direct message given verbally; or, through an inner mental impulse, the writer's mind being intellectually or emotionally impelled to write, or, through a general rational illumination, reason having been enlightened by experience. I find that the inspired writings fall into categories involving one or two of these methods of inspiration."

"Well," said Cynthia Moore, "in spite of what Jack said about dictation, I must point out that the giving of the Ten Commandments to Moses—read in Exodus, chapter twenty—was dictation."

"I agree," replied Michael Stratton-Smith. "That is one of these varieties of inspiration. Within this divine inspiration, we recognize—first, an outer verbal revelation without any inner mental impulse. That's the first category."

"How about the introduction to the Book of the Revelation?" asked Jerry Jansen. "John the divine heard a voice but also received some sort of inner mental impulse."

"Very well," replied Michael. "We'll call that the

second category, an outer verbal revelation with an inner mental impulse."

"Then what about the prologue to the Gospel of Luke?" asked Rafferty Jones. " 'Inasmuch as many have undertaken to compile a narrative of the things which have been accomplished among us, just as they were delivered to us by those who from the beginning were eyewitnesses and ministers of the Word, it seemed good to me also, having followed all things closely for some time past, to write an orderly account for you, most excellent Theophilus, that you may know the truth concerning the things of which you have been informed.' "

"That sounds as if Dr. Luke was compiling a narrative by consulting those who knew," said Helen Johnson.

"We'll call that category three," said Michael. "Third, an inner mental impulse, without any outer verbal revelation whatsoever."

"I have always been puzzled," said Rafferty Jones, "over the advice given by the apostle Paul to the married and the unmarried in the First Letter to the Corinthians, chapter seven. He says 'I say this by way of concession and not of command' and 'I give my opinion as one that is trustworthy.' What does this mean?"

"I have always understood," replied Jansen, "that the apostle was expressing an enlightened opinion, disclaiming that he had received either a direct message or an inner impulse. The advice he gave to married couples still stands. The advice to the unmarried to remain single was in view of the outbreak of terrible persecution."

"Let's call this the fourth category," said Michael. "How shall we put it? Fourth, a conscious rational illumination without an inner mental impulse."

"What about the apostle Paul's comments in the second chapter of that Epistle?" asked Weber. "'We impart this in words not taught by human wisdom, but taught by the Spirit, interpreting spiritual truths to those who possess the Spirit.'"

"We'll call that category five," said Michael. "Fifth, a conscious rational illumination with an inner mental impulse."

"I have found a real mystery," said Cynthia. "The apostle Peter in his First Letter, chapter one, says that the prophets inquired what person or time was indicated by the Spirit of Christ in them when predicting the suffering and glory of Christ. It was revealed to them that they were serving not themselves but us. Now what does this mean?"

"It means that the Old Testament prophets in prophesying about Christ," explained MacNeill, "did not themselves understand the prophecy, which was meant for us in later generations."

"Let's call this category six," said Michael. "Sixth, an inner mental impulse, without any conscious rational illumination."

Chapter 20

DID GOD
DICTATE THE BIBLE?

"**W**e must continue our discussion," said the Chaplain, "regarding the Bible."

"Let me ask," said P. T. Liu, "whether you think that the Bible is wholly a divine book? How much of the book is human?"

"Of course, it is human," said Phil.

"But how much?"

"It is human literature, divinely inspired."

"There are many human elements in the text," answered Ted Bond. "As we read the Authorized Version in its quaint Elizabethan English, we think that it is all of one style. But reading in the original languages or in modern translations soon clears away that idea. Take a simple example. The apostle Paul had an academic style whereas the apostle Peter had a simple style. Whoever wrote the Epistle to the Hebrews had an exquisite style."

"What other human devices are there?"

"There are figures of speech in the Bible," said Helen Johnson. "For example, the Gospel claims that when John the Baptist was preaching in the wilderness, all Judea went out to hear him. To take that literally, one would have to say that every man, woman, youth, maid, boy, girl, baby and baby-sitter went out!"

"There are symbols in the Bible," added Phil Weber. "It speaks in the Book of Revelation of one-hundred-and-forty-four thousand. Leaders of one cult taught for a long time that they were the hundred-and-forty-four thousand saved, until their numbers passed that figure, after which they changed their interpretation. Obviously, the figure is symbolical. Twelve is the number of perfection, and one thousand is the number of multitude, so a perfectly perfect multitude of people will be saved."

"The Scripture also contains history, poetry, drama, allegory, proverbs and the like," said Jerry Jansen. "These are legitimate literary devices used by humans."

"We can sum up by saying," added Michael, "that the Spirit of God obviously allowed writers a latitude of style, and use of figures of speech and symbols."

"How are we to know which is which?" asked Pat Bonelli. "Which is narrative, symbolism, history, or poetry?"

"Augustine declared," replied Michael, "that 'Scripture is what Scripture means,' and that is a good reason for Bible study."

"Plain narrative must be treated as history, and poems treated as poetry," commented Phil Weber, "while figures of speech may not be taken as technical details or symbols taken literally."

The Chaplain summed it up.

"One must avoid the extremes of taking every phrase literally and taking passages allegorically out of all context," said he.

"Why," asked P. T. Liu, "do differences of interpretation of Scripture exist between various Christians?"

"Some differences in the interpretation of the Scriptures are due to human prejudice," added the Chaplain, "and others to ignorance, some to one-sidedness and others to farfetched ideas, not a few to poor principles of interpretation."

"Why are there difficulties of interpretation of Scripture that no Christians can resolve?"

"In the Scriptures are found copyists' errors, both solved and unsolved," explained MacNeill, "not one of which affects the understanding of the way of salvation."

"There are expressions of ancient thinking," added Petersen, "and misunderstood texts, the language of accommodation and the problems of various kinds."

"That's hard on an ordinary reader like me," objected Bonelli.

"Oh, no," replied Jansen. "Encountering an occasional problem does not rob the reader of profit in reading what is so plainly understood by all and besides, further light may explain what presently is hard to comprehend. Until one obeys the light that he possesses, further light is very seldom given."

"The Bible," said the Chaplain, "is a book of literary grandeur. Yet it is a model of simplicity. It is dramatic. It is poetic. Writers find it difficult to hide themselves in their own writings, yet the writers of the Bible succeeded in so doing that in some instances nobody knows who or how many wrote a given book.

"Our English Bible is a masterpiece of pure prose. It is a classic. Yet the Bible has been translated into many other languages equally well. It becomes part of the literature of every people presented with it.

"The biographical sketches of the Bible are unique. There is no flattery, and yet there is no depressing influence in its faithful denunciation of sinners and their sinful ways. And in the Bible men have found the inspiration to change not only their individual lives but the lives of nations.

"The Bible is an incomparable book. It is a book with a sublime influence, a book with an unusual unity, a book of extraordinary accuracy and a book which is full of life.

"In very truth, it is a revelation of God."

Chapter 21

WHAT IS GOD LIKE?

"I came to this class," said Pat Bonelli, "as a critic, in fact an unbeliever. I must say that I appreciate the way that the ideas and doctrines are being presented to us. As I see it," he went on, "we have been establishing the Scriptures as the source of our authority for what we are to learn about God, seeing that science cannot tell us anything. So, where do we go from here?"

"What does the Scripture reveal to us about God?" asked Julio Vasconceles.

The question was thrown out to the class.

" 'God is spirit,' " suggested Cynthia Moore, " 'and those who worship him must worship him in spirit and truth.' John chapter four, verse twenty-four."

"Very well," said the Chaplain. "We agree that Scripture reveals first, the spirituality of God."

"His infinity," suggested Harry McClelland. "From Solomon's prayer in the First Book of Kings, chapter eight, verse twenty-seven: 'the heaven of heavens cannot contain Thee.'"

"Fine," said the Chaplain. "Scripture reveals second, the infinity of God."

"His perfection," suggested Hernando Garcia. "'Your heavenly Father is perfect.' I cannot tell where that is in the Holy Bible, but it was said by Jesus."

"Matthew chapter five, verse forty-eight," prompted Jerry Jansen.

"Excellent," said the Chaplain. "Scripture reveals third, the perfection of God. Spirituality, infinity and perfection. Obviously, science could not tell us these things. The Scripture 'attributes' certain characteristics of the divine nature to God which theology designates the attributes of God, either absolute or relative to his creation."

"How are these absolute attributes of God stated?" asked Nils Andersson.

"Scripture ascribes to God as the attributes of spirituality," answered Michael, "first, life; second, energy; and third, personality."

"References?" asked Charles Fitzgerald, in making notes.

"Well," said Michael, "Jeremiah, in chapter ten and verse ten, speaks of the living God—that's life. In his First Epistle chapter one, verse five, the apostle John tells us that God is light—that's energy. And God himself told Moses, Exodus, chapter three, verse fourteen, to tell the children of Israel 'I AM hath sent me to you'—and that's personality."

"All three refer to spirituality," said Bonelli. "What about infinity?"

Michael looked around and Jerry Jansen took up the theme of infinity.

"Scripture ascribes to God as the attributes of infinity," he stated, "first, self-existence; second, unchangeableness; and third, unity."

"References?"

"Well," said Jerry. "Exodus chapter three, verse fourteen, speaks of 'I AM THAT I AM'—that's self-existence. In Malachi chapter three, verse six, it declares 'I the Lord change not'—that's unchangeableness. And in Deuteronomy chapter six, verse four, 'Hear, O Israel, the Lord our God is one Lord'—that's unity."

"Okay," commented Petersen. "We have now dealt with spirituality and infinity. What about perfection?"

"Scripture ascribes to God as the attributes of perfection," said Ted Bond, "first, truth; second, love; and third, holiness."

"References?"

"Well," said Ted. "Doesn't it say in John's Gospel, chapter seventeen, verse three, 'the only true God'? —that's truth. Then we all know the reference in the First Epistle of John, chapter four, verse eight, 'God is love'—that's love. And in the prophecy of Isaiah, chapter six, verse three, is the ascription 'Holy, holy, holy is the Lord of Hosts'—that's holiness."

"This is tough going," commented Petersen.

"There is only one thing to do," said Weber, "and that is to master it. Let's see if I have gotten it right. Scripture reveals the spirituality and infinity and perfection of God—that's easy to remember, a trio. God's spirituality itself is threefold—life, energy and personality. God's infinity itself is threefold —self-existence and unchangeableness and unity. And God's holiness itself is threefold—truth and love and holiness. That's not so hard. A trio of trios to

133

remember. And they all are absolute attributes of God."

"What do you mean, absolute?" asked Helen.

"I suppose," said Rafferty Jones, "that these attributes are absolute in God himself without reference to anyone or anything else, whereas the relative attributes are in reference to finite beings and things."

"What does Scripture ascribe to God then," asked Julio, "in relation to his material, animal and spiritual creation, as relative attributes?"

"Michael?" prompted the Chaplain.

"Let me see, let me see!" said the Englishman. "The relative attributes of God are stated in Scripture in relation to the material universe, in relation to all living creatures, and in relation to moral beings.

"First, in relation to the material universe, as (one) immensity, (two) eternity and (three) incorporeality. References? For immensity, I would quote again the passage from the First Book of Kings chapter eight, verse twenty-seven, 'the heaven of heavens cannot contain Thee.' For eternity, I would quote the Ninetieth Psalm verse 'from everlasting . . . Thou art God.' And for incorporeality —meaning, not being limited to a body—I would quote Colossians, chapter one, verse fifteen, regarding 'the invisible God.' "

"Immense! Eternal! Incorporeal!" P. T. Liu repeated. "New words to an engineer, but I am learning theology now."

"Second, in relation to all living creatures," Stratton-Smith went on, "the relative attributes of God given in Scripture are (one) omnipotence, (two)

134

omniscience and (three) omnipresence, which are lacking in animals, men and angels."

"Please define those words," asked Cynthia.

"God is omnipotent," replied Fritz Wagner, "which means that he is all-powerful. God is omniscient which means that he is all-knowing. And God is omnipresent, which means that he is everywhere present."

Wagner seemed rather pleased that he, an anthropologist, was following a theological discussion.

"Okay," said David Adams. "Can Michael give us the details from the Scripture?"

"Most assuredly," said Michael. "In Genesis chapter seventeen, verse one, it begins 'I am God Almighty'—that's omnipotence. In Hebrews, the fourth chapter, verse thirteen, it says 'all things are open to His eyes'—that's omniscience. And in Jeremiah chapter twenty-three, verse twenty-four, the question 'Do not I fill heaven and earth?'—that's omnipresence."

"All right," said Pat Bonelli. "You have a third section to give us.

"Yes," replied Michael. "Third, in relation to moral beings, the relative attributes of God revealed in Scripture are (one) truthfulness and faithfulness; (two) mercy and goodness; and (three) justice and righteousness. References? 'Let God be true and every man a liar,' Romans chapter four, verse three and 'God is faithful,' First Corinthians chapter one, verse nine for truthfulness and faithfulness; 'I trust in the mercy of God,' Psalm fifty-two, verse eight and 'the goodness of God,' Romans chapter two, verse four for mercy and goodness; and 'Shall not the Judge of all the earth do right?' Genesis chapter eighteen, verse twenty-five and 'The Lord is righteous,' in Lamentations chapter one, verse eighteen for justice and righteousness."

There were sighs of relief as the members of the class heard Michael conclude.

"I hope," said the Chaplain, "that you have all been making notes of these references. This is not merely a technical theological discussion of the attributes of God. Before very long, you will see the application that we are going to make of what we have learned about God from the Holy Scriptures. Let's grant it, this was tough going, but it was well worth while."

Rafferty Jones promised his Zulu friend to go over the material with him again.

Chapter 22

HOW CAN THERE BE
THREE IN ONE?

"If you don't mind," said the Chaplain, "we shall recapitulate the lessons of our previous discussion. Our reasons for studying the attributes of God were not academic but practical."

"To whom does the Scripture ascribe the attributes of Deity? That is the question," said Stratton-Smith.

"The first thing that occurs to me," said Pat Bonelli, "is that it is not our purpose to establish the doctrine of the Deity of Almighty God. That goes without saying. Therefore, our purpose must be to establish a doctrine of the Deity of Christ."

"Why should that be necessary?"

"Well," replied Bonelli, "I have heard people say that Jesus Christ was only an ordinary man who possessed more of God in degree than other people. I have heard other people say that he became the Son of God by adoption at baptism. I have heard the propagandists of an odd cult say that he was a created angelic being, but not truly Deity. And I have heard the advocates of another odd sect say that Jesus was the man and Christ was the idea in his mind, whatever that means. Sure, this is going to be an interesting session for me. The figure of Jesus Christ towers over all of history."

"Very well," said the Chaplain. "Let us take our questions in order. To whom does Scripture ascribe the attributes of Deity?"

"May I answer that?" asked Stratton-Smith. "This is the orthodox view, and I believe it may be clearly proven. Scripture, as we shall see, attributes Deity not to angels, not to men, but only to the eternal Father, to the eternal Son, and to the eternal Spirit, a trinity in unity."

"Hold on," said David Adams. "I heard a lecturer announce that the word 'trinity' does not occur anywhere in the Bible."

"Quite," replied Michael. "The doctrine of the Trinity is not formally stated in Scripture. This truth is intimated in the Old Testament and clearly revealed in the New, though the formal word 'trinity' is not used in either."

"I have a question," said Zefani Mhlongwa. "Does the 'trinity in unity' mean that there are three Gods?"

"Certainly not," replied Harry McClelland. "Scripture teaches that there is one God but it indicates that there are three eternal distinctions in the nature of God which, for the lack of a better word, we designate as 'persons.'"

"In India," said S. S. Ramakrishna, "we also worship a 'trinity' of Brahma, Vishnu and Shiva. I do not find the idea difficult."

"With all due respect, Mr. Ramakrishna," said the Chaplain, "I disagree with you about the Christian doctrine of the Trinity. This is not to be compared with tri-theism in other religions."

The Chaplain spoke so strongly that eyebrows were raised.

"Oh, Chaplain," said Cynthia Moore. "I am sure that S. S. knows what he is talking about."

"No, sir," said the Chaplain again. "There is no similarity between the Christian Trinity of God the Father, Son and Spirit and the ideas of Hinduism worshiping as deity Brahma, Vishnu and Shiva —'gods' that quarrel and fight and indulge in the passions that mankind repudiates. No, sir."

"Perhaps there is a difference," conceded the Indian, courteously and with the Hindu facility for seeing two sides of a question. "But is there not a similarity between the Lord Krishna and the Lord Christ? I have often heard that said in our discussions in India."

The Chaplain did not reply. Lt. Jack Petersen spoke up. "No offense meant, sir," he said. "But from my acquaintance with the Lord Krishna, I would say that his character was midway between Robin Hood and Errol Flynn."

"Returning to the subject of the Trinity," said the Chaplain, indicating that the discussion of alien gods was ended. "What are the intimations in the Old Testament of the threefold nature of Almighty God?"

"I was not aware that the Old Testament anywhere referred to the Trinity," said Bonelli.

"The Old Testament Scripture," began Phil Weber, "uses a plural noun and plural verb in Hebrew referring to God, and a plural pronoun where God is speaking of himself."

"References?"

"Well, for example," replied Weber, "in the twentieth chapter of Genesis, verse thirteen, the patriarch Abraham declared that 'God caused me to wander from my father's house.' The verb 'caused' is in the plural as well as the noun. And in the thirty-fifth chapter, verse seven, Jacob built the altar of Bethel 'because there God was revealed to him'—the same plural construction.

"The references for the plural pronoun used by the Lord in speaking of himself are numerous. 'Let us make man in our image'—Genesis chapter one, verse twenty-six; 'the man is become one of us'—Genesis chapter three, verse twenty-two; 'Let us go down and confound their language'—Genesis chapter eleven, verse seven; and from the prophecy of Isaiah, chapter six, verse eight, 'Whom shall I send, and who will go for us?' "

There was a lengthy pause as the class took this in. Then Helen Johnson protested: "Well, then, why don't other people see this clearly? What is their objection to this?"

"They say," said Stratton-Smith, "that this use of the plural is what we call the 'royal plural' or the 'editorial plural.' They have a point. But remember what the Chaplain said. These are intimations of doctrine, not clear statements."

"Just keep in mind," said Jerry Jansen, "the Christian view is that the doctrine of the Trinity in unity was hidden until the revelation of Christ. It is only intimated in the Old Testament.'

"What other references are there?"

"Old Testament Scripture refers to the Son of God and the Spirit of God, clearly," added Michael.

"Where?"

"In Psalm two, verse seven, and in Proverbs chapter thirty, verse four, referring to the Son of God. Referring to the Spirit of God, Genesis chapter one, verses one and two; Isaiah chapter sixty-three, verse ten. There are others."

"This is all new to me," said Bonelli.

"There is a threefold divine ascription," said Ted Bond, "and a threefold divine benediction in the Old Testament. 'Holy, holy, holy' in Isaiah chapter six, verse three; and in Numbers chapter six, verses twenty-four, -five and -six, 'The Lord bless thee and keep thee: the Lord make His face to shine upon thee and be gracious unto thee: the Lord lift up His countenance upon thee and give thee peace.'"

"What troubles me," said Charles Fitzgerald, "is why this mystery, that's what I call it, this mystery of the Godhead should have been kept secret for thousands of years, then revealed."

"There is this to remember, Charles," said Jerry Jansen, "that the Old Testament clearly predicted the coming of a remarkable person, the Messiah, or Christ, or Anointed One. And it follows that the logical time for the disclosure of this mystery was that coming of the Messiah, more especially as the Old Testament invested him with extraordinary attributes."

"Does the Old Testament ascribe attributes of Deity to the predicted Messiah?" asked Liu.

"It is obvious," said Harry McClelland, "that the Hebrew people thought of the Messiah as a great national Deliverer. But the Scriptures said more than that about him."

"Like what?"

"The Old Testament indicates," said Michael, "that the Messiah is one with God the Father in the prophecy of Isaiah: 'for His name shall be called Wonderful, Counselor, Mighty God, Everlasting Father and Prince of Peace'—surely the titles of divine majesty, in chapter nine, verse six. The same is true in the prophecy of Micah concerning Bethlehem, 'His goings forth are from of old, from days of eternity'—surely referring to Messiah's timeless existence, in the fifth chapter, verse two—quoting the Berkeley Version. These are the Messianic prophecies."

"And yet," said Houston MacNeill, "Messiah is made in some sense distinct from the Father, as the Psalmist says 'Thy throne, O God, is for ever and ever . . . therefore God, thy God, hath anointed thee . . .'"

"All I can say," commented David Adams, "is that this is difficult to understand."

"Yes. Only the New Testament doctrine of the Deity of Christ explains these references," said Jerry Jansen.

"We must leave New Testament references until our next discussion," said the Chaplain.

"Do you know," said Cynthia Moore, "while I always believed that Jesus is the Son of God, it is only just now that I'm beginning to understand the Christmas carol:

'There's a tumult of joy
'O'er the wonderful birth;
'For the Virgin's sweet boy
'Is the Lord of the earth.'"

Chapter 23

HOW CAN THREE BE ONE?

"**L**ast session," said P. T. Liu, "it was said that the doctrine of the Trinity is intimated in the Old Testament. Is it taught clearly in the New? Does the New Testament speak of Father, Son and Spirit as a 'trinity in unity'?"

"It was said before," replied Stratton-Smith, "that the doctrine is stated clearly but not formally. In other words, the New Testament does not say that God exists as a 'trinity in unity.' It does however speak of the Father, Son and Holy Spirit together in equal terms. And it ascribes Deity to the Father, Son and Holy Spirit in clear terms separately. Suppose we study this?"

"Following Michael's statement," said Jerry Jansen, "I am making a simple proposition. The number of combinations of three symbols a,b,c, is six —abc, acb, bca, bac, cab, and cba. Right? Let's see if the New Testament makes the six combinations. Write down 'Father, Son, Spirit' and so on in all possible combinations of order. Then each try to locate a verse to match them."

"I'll begin," said Cynthia Moore. "The New Testament speaks first, of the Father, Son and Spirit in the baptismal formula; that reference is in Matthew's Gospel, chapter twenty-eight, verse nineteen."

There was a long pause before McClelland proposed the second reference.

"In the First Epistle of Peter," he said, "in chapter one, verse two, it speaks second, of the Father, Spirit and Son in the election of saints; this is a clear statement."

"What do you mean?" asked P. T. Liu. "The election of saints. How do they elect saints?"

Harry McClelland's jaw dropped. He looked at the verse in his Authorized Version, and then despaired of interpreting it to a former Buddhist.

"Read it in a modern translation, Harry," said Rafferty Jones. "This one puts it that true Christians are chosen by God the Father, set apart by the Spirit and cleansed by the Son."

There was another long pause before the third combination was noticed.

"Here it is," said Jerry Jansen. "Hebrews chapter nine, verse fourteen, speaks third, of the Son, Spirit and Father in the atonement; so look it up, Peetee."

Zefani Mhlongwa was ready with the fourth.

"The apostle Paul," he said enthusiastically, "speaks fourth, of the Son, Father and Spirit in the —what you say?—the benediction. That is the Second Letter to the Corinthians, chapter thirteen, verse fourteen."

"I know that one," said P. T. Liu, equally enthusiastically, while Ramakrishna added, "And I also have heard that one in India."

There was a longer pause still before someone volunteered the fifth proposition.

"I have found it," said Michael. "In John's Gospel, chapter fifteen, verse twenty-six, it is speaking fifth, of the Spirit, Father and Son in the promise of the Paraclete, the Comforter."

"Please excuse," interrupted Julio.

"It's a Greek word," said the Chaplain. "In your Portuguese Bible, it is almost the same word 'Quando vier o Paraclito . . .' The English word is Comforter, an obsolete translation."

"That leaves the sixth," said Jerry Jansen. "I have a suggestion, but I'll wait to see if anyone else has a better one."

No one responded.

"In the First Epistle to the Corinthians," said Jerry, "it speaks sixth, of the Spirit, Son and Father in the donation of spiritual gifts to the Church. And the same order is given in the baptism of the Lord Jesus in Jordan."

"Well," said Nils Andersson. "What are we trying to prove?"

"These six forms," replied Weber, "exhaust the possibilities of order of mention, and emphasize the essential equality of the Father, the Son and the Spirit in the Godhead."

There was another pause.

"I'm beginning to see," said Fitzgerald. "You mean, if the Blessed Virgin Mary were on a plane of equality with Christ, we should expect equal mention in the plan of salvation."

"You can take this for what it is worth," said McClelland. "These trinitarian formulae cited in support refer to election, atonement, baptism, commission, equipment and enduement. That is surely an involvement of the Father, Son and Spirit in the plan of salvation, as Charlie said."

"Is this the total argument for the Trinity in the New Testament?" asked Garcia.

"Oh, no," replied Jansen. "This is just a preliminary mention of the trinitarian formula. There is much more reference to the Deity of Christ and the Deity of the Holy Spirit."

"My friends," said the Chaplain, seriously, "if you are finding the doctrine of God far from easy to grasp, do not let that discourage you. I would like to ask you frankly: Do you comprehend the doctrine of the Trinity?"

There was dead silence.

Zefani Mhlongwa, the Zulu student, spoke up, to encourage the Chaplain, no doubt. Said he, "Sir, I am beginning to comprehend it."

The Chaplain smiled. "Zefani, I contend that no man can comprehend the doctrine of the Trinity. Listen. If you could fully comprehend the doctrine of God, then God would not be any greater than the scope of your intelligence."

"But, sir," Zefani protested. "How then can anyone understand anything about God?"

"Zefani," said the Chaplain, "we can only understand what God has chosen to reveal to us, and he has revealed himself to us as Father, Son and Spirit, one God. Let's keep this in mind. The term 'trinity' is not a metaphysical one. It is only a designation of four facts: first, that the Father is God; second, the Son is God; third, the Spirit is God; and fourth, there is one God."

"Could someone set me right about illustrating

146

the doctrine of the Trinity?" asked Jerry Jansen. "I hear the most ridiculous analogies."

"My Sunday School teacher," said Cynthia, "used the illustration of an egg being composed of shell, white and yolk. That didn't sound right, though I don't know why."

"Don't know why!" said Helen. "The yolk is fat, the white is albumen and the shell is calcium and there is no essential unity there."

"My Bible Class leader," said Rafferty Jones, "used the illustration of water, existing in three forms, ice, water and steam."

"That one lacks the essential threeness," said Nils Andersson. "Ice, water and steam are one compound, and one form may be converted into another. That falls short, too."

"My pastor," said Helen Johnson, "spoke of himself as a father to his family, a pastor to his church and a citizen to his state. How's that?"

"I say," exclaimed Michael Stratton-Smith. "Your pastor would be shocked to know that he was a heretic on this point. The heresy of the Sabellians was condemned in the third century. It was the idea that Father, Son and Spirit are three characters or modes or relations of the Godhead, in other words, God acting in three different parts. We have already shown that the Son of God is eternal."

"Well," said David Adams, "what is your analogy, Michael?"

"I doubt there is one," replied he. "Are there analogies in nature of the Trinity in unity? The perfect analogy must stress first, an essential threeness in oneness, second, of being and not of doing, and third, an orderly relationship."

"Speaking as a scientist," said Andersson, "the

closest analogies would be those of space, time and matter in the universe; of length, width, depth, in space; of future, present and past in time; or of energy, motion and phenomena in matter. Everything in the universe has length, width and depth, imaginary things like the point, line, and such, geometry notwithstanding. And all events are future, present or past from some point of view. And so on."

"Even then," said the Chaplain. "The mystery of God is beyond all. It is easier to use the triunity of God to explain the trinities in nature than vice versa."

Chapter 24

ARE JESUS AND GOD EQUAL?

"Let us see further," said the Chaplain, "to whom the New Eestament ascribes Deity."

"Is Deity ascribed in the New Testament to the Father?" asked Zefani Mhlongwa.

"The New Testament ascribes Deity to the Father in many passages," replied Ted Bond, "of which one speaks of 'the foreknowledge of God the Father.' That's from the First Epistle of Peter, chapter one, verse two."

"I don't understand this," said Cynthia. "Why should we look for references to the Deity of God the Father. He is God, isn't he?"

"Yes, of course," said the Chaplain. "He is God. Often the Scripture refers to him as the Father to distinguish him from the Spirit or the Son, who are likewise God."

"All right," said Cynthia. "I can see that now. Let us go on."

149

"Is Deity ascribed in the New Testament to the Holy Spirit?" asked Helen Johnson.

"Yes," said Julio Vasconceles. "The New Testament speaks of the Holy Spirit as God in the story of Ananias and Sapphira."

"Yes," repeated Ted Bond. "The Scripture ascribes to the Holy Spirit the attributes of a personality, intellect, will and emotion."

"References, please?"

"In John's Gospel," replied Ted, "chapter fourteen, verse twenty-six, it speaks of his own ability to teach us all things. In the Acts of the Apostles, chapter sixteen, verses six and seven, we find that the Spirit of God restrained Paul and Silas in their ministry, and directed them elsewhere. In Ephesians chapter four, verse thirty, there is the well-known exhortation 'Grieve not the Holy Spirit.' These references witness to the intellect, will and emotion of the Spirit."

"There are other arguments," said Michael. "We have agreed that omnipotence, omniscience and omnipresence are attributes of Deity, and you will find all three attributed to the Spirit of God. He helped create the world—Genesis one, verse two—that's omnipotence; He knows the thoughts of God—First Corinthians, chapter two, verses ten and eleven—that's omniscience; and He is everywhere present—Psalm one-hundred-thirty-nine, verse seven—that's omnipresence."

"And," said Weber, "Scripture ascribes to the Holy Spirit the absolute attribute of life, in Romans chapter eight, verse two; the absolute attribute of self-existence, in Hebrews chapter nine, verse fourteen; and the absolutes of truth, and love and holiness, in John's Gospel chapter sixteen, verse thirteen; Romans chapter fifteen, verse thirty; and Ephesians chapter four, verse thirty. These are attributes of Deity."

"Is Deity ascribed in the New Testament to the Son?" asked Fritz Wagner.

"Yes," replied Houston MacNeill. "The New Testament ascribes Deity to Jesus Christ as the eternal Son in the introduction of the Gospel of John, chapter one, verse one, 'and the Word was God'—herein using a word for absolute Deity."

"Hold on," said David Adams. "I had a long discussion with a fellow who put his foot in my door and wouldn't go away. He read from his version of the Bible and it said something like this, 'In the beginning was the Word, and the Word was with God, and the Word was a god.'"

The Chaplain intervened.

"I had a letter the other day," he explained, "from my old professor of New Testament Greek who, by the way, is co-author of a much-used university-level Grammar of Koine Greek. We were referring to the fact that the cultists you mention cite his Grammar in support of their perversion of the Greek text. My old professor indignantly repudiated them. No, you can read the Greek this way: 'In the beginning was the Word, and the Word was with God, and the Word was Deity.' The word for Deity in that phrase is 'theos' without an article. Be assured that this use is for absolute Deity, not the divinity of men or angels. This verse teaches Christ's timeless existence, and his personal existence, and his essential nature as God."

"It is interesting," commented Jansen, "that cultists who believe that a use of 'theos' without the article refers to something less than Deity must manipulate another verse differently, one that uses 'theos' with the article speaking of the Lord Jesus. The apostle Thomas ascribed Deity to the risen Christ who fully accepted the honor as recorded in John's Gospel, chapter twenty, verse twenty-eight, 'My Lord and my God!' "

"Yes," said Stratton-Smith, "and the apostle Paul wrote of the glory of 'our great God and Saviour Jesus Christ' in his Letter to Titus, in chapter two, verse thirteen. I am quoting from your American Revised Standard Version which is much more accurate here than our Authorized Version, the King James you call it, which is a bit ambiguous at this point."

"How's that?" said Harry McClelland.

"Look it up, old boy! Look it up!"

Harry looked it up and compared it, to his own mild astonishment.

"Does the New Testament apply Old Testament references to God to Jesus Christ?" asked Rafferty Jones. "I seem to remember somebody saying so."

"Yes," replied Michael. "I remember the references. The New Testament quotes Isaiah's phrase 'the way of the Lord'—chapter forty, and verse three—and clearly applies it to Christ in Matthew, chapter three, verse three. The same is true of Isaiah's vision of the glory of the Lord—in chapter six, verse one—clearly applied to Christ in John, chapter twelve, verse forty-one."

"And," added Jerry Jansen, "there is a clear reference in Hebrews, chapter one, verse six, to Psalm ninety-seven, verse seven, in which it says 'all ye gods, worship Him'—these 'gods' referring to the angelic rulers and so quoted as 'angels of God' in Hebrews."

"Hold on, there," said David Adams. "The fellow that put his foot in my door and wouldn't go away said something about God and gods. Is not the designation 'god' in a lower sense used of angels and men in Scripture?"

"The words 'god' or 'gods' are used rarely in Scripture of angelic and human rulers," said Michael, "but it is always in a manner which indicates a rhetorical and not a literal sense. Your friend put his foot in his mouth as well as in the door by trying to prove that the eternal Son of God was only an archangel, for the Epistle to the Colossians in chapter one, verse sixteen, declares that the Son of God created all the host of angels. He was Deity."

"In the same connection," added Fitzgerald, "Jesus Christ said 'I and the Father are one' and 'He that hath seen Me hath seen the Father.' The references are both in the Gospel of John, in chapter ten, verse thirty and chapter fourteen, verse nine."

"You should have heard the fellow who put his foot in my door and wouldn't go away try to get around those verses," said David Adams. "He said that Jesus nowhere claimed equality with God. He quoted some verses showing his subordination."

"Did Jesus Christ himself claim an equality with God the Father?" asked Nils Andersson.

"The New Testament states his claims to equality simply," replied Michael. "I know that David's doorstep debater would try to explain that Jesus must have meant something else when he spoke of his relationship to the Father, but in John's Gospel, chapter five, verse eighteen, it states that the Jews sought all the more to kill him 'because ... He said also that God was His Father, making Himself equal with God'—so it is certain that his critics did not misunderstand his meaning."

"There is another verse," said Phil. "'Who being in the form of God, thought it not robbery to be equal with God.' He held equality as a right. The reference is Philippians, chapter two, verse six, I think."

David Adams felt that his question was still unanswered. He repeated it.

"Does the New Testament teach that Christ was inferior or subordinate to God the Father?"

The Chaplain answered. "Certain New Testament passages impute to Christ a lack of strength and knowledge. 'Jesus being wearied with his journey sat by the well,' John, chapter four, verse six, speaks of his true humanity. Mark, chapter thirteen, verse thirty-two—'But of that day or that hour no one knows, not even the angels in heaven, nor the Son, but only the Father'—speaks of something hidden from him in his humanity.

"Perhaps the answer to this mystery lies in attributing the limitation and subjection of Jesus to the humiliation of Christ in his incarnation. Philippians, chapter two, verse seven, states that he emptied himself, taking the form of a servant—like Bonnie Prince Charlie disguising himself as the serving-man of Flora MacDonald. This verse teaches that his divine nature was in some way both limited and humbled during his earthly life. That's why he said 'the Father is greater than I'—John, chapter fourteen, verse twenty-eight. There seems to be order of office and operation in the Godhead consistent with Christ's equality with God. It is a mystery of incarnation."

Chapter 25

SO, WHAT'S THE ANSWER?

"Let us conclude our study of the attributes of Deity ascribed to Christ," said Michael.

"Does the New Testament apply to the Lord Jesus the absolute attributes of God?" asked Pat Bonelli.

"I thought we answered that," said Michael.

"No, we didn't," replied MacNeill, "and yes—it does. The New Testament ascribes to Jesus Christ the divine attributes of life — 'in Him was life,' found in the Gospel of John chapter one, verse four; and self-existence—found in Hebrews chapter seven, verse sixteen, which says that in Christ is the power of an endless life; and unchangeableness—found in the same book, chapter thirteen, verse six, 'Jesus Christ, the same yesterday, today and forever.' "

"Quite so," said Michael. "There are also declarations of his attributes of truth, love and holiness.

References? John chapter fourteen, verse six; First Epistle of John chapter three, verse sixteen; and John chapter six, verse sixty-nine. These are attributes of Deity."

"You mentioned relative attributes, too, is it not?" asked Hernando Garcia. "What are such attributes, the relative attributes of the Son?" He followed the discussion despite his language handicaps.

"That is equally clear," replied McClelland. "The New Testament attributes to Jesus Christ the attribute of eternity, for which I will give four references—'before Abraham was, I am,' found in John chapter eight, verse fifty-eight; 'the glory I had with Thee before the world was,' found in John chapter seventeen and verse five; 'in the beginning was the Word,' found in John chapter one, verse one; and 'I am the Alpha and the Omega, the beginning and the end,' found in Revelation chapter twenty-one, verse six."

"This is astounding," commented P. T. Liu.

"You haven't heard everything yet," said Phil Weber. "It ascribed to him omnipotence—I'll give double references, Matthew chapter twenty-eight, verse twenty and Revelation chapter one, verse eight; omniscience—John chapter two, verses twenty-four and twenty-five and Colossians chapter two, verse three; and omnipresence—Matthew chapter twenty-eight, verse twenty and Ephesians chapter one, verse twenty-three."

"Let's read these references," said Cynthia.

The group shared them.

" 'All power is given unto Me in heaven and on earth.' 'I am Alpha and Omega . . . the Almighty.' 'Jesus knew all men and . . . knew what was in man.' 'In whom are hid all the treasures of wisdom and knowledge.' 'I am with you alway, even unto the end of the world.' 'The fulness of Him who filleth all in all.' "

"Does the New Testament teach the Deity of Christ in other phrases?" asked Helen Johnson. "Have we exhausted the arguments?"

"The Deity of Christ," said Sam MacNeill, "is taught in the phrases 'the Image of God' and 'the Son of God'—the first in Colossians chapter one, verse fifteen and the second in the Gospel of Matthew chapter twenty-six and verse sixty-three, the latter claim being regarded as blasphemy by the Jews."

"Are the works of God ascribed to the Son?" asked Petersen, and Ted Bond answered.

"The New Testament ascribes to Jesus Christ the work of Creation," he said emphatically. "I think the reference is in the Epistle to the Colossians chapter one, verse sixteen, which says that 'all things have been created through Him.' Creation is the work of God."

"Not only so," said Michael Stratton-Smith, "but the writer of the Epistle to the Hebrews ascribes to Jesus Christ the work of upholding that creation —'upholding all things by the word of His power,' which is found in chapter one, verse three."

"I don't know if this follows in series," said Harry. "The Gospel of John ascribes a work of God to the Lord Jesus, in his own words, the work of judgment—'authority to execute judgment' which other passages extend to judging the whole world."

"Are we agreed that Scripture ascribes to Christ the works of God?" asked the Chaplain.

There was nodded assent.

"Very well, then. Does the New Testament offer to Jesus Christ the honor and worship and glory due to God alone?"

"My answer to all three points is yes," said Jerry Jansen. "The New Testament offers honor and worship and glory to Jesus Christ—first, 'that all may honor the Son, even as they honor the Father' which is found in the Gospel of John chapter five, verse twenty-three; second, 'that at the name of Jesus every knee should bow . . .' which is found in the Epistle to the Philippians chapter two, verse ten; and 'to whom be the glory for ever and ever' which is found in Hebrews chapter thirteen, verse twenty-one. In view of the fact that the Jews were so strict regarding the blasphemy of human claims to Deity, these statements recorded by writers of Jewish birth are all the more remarkable."

The members of the class found themselves looking at one another. P. T. Liu seemed to be struggling with deep emotion. He stood to his feet. In a quiet voice, he said:

"I believe that Jesus is the Christ, the Son of the living God, the Saviour of the world. I have found peace."

Cynthia Moore failed to keep back her tears.